K. A. BUSIA ON AFRICA

Volume 2

PURPOSEFUL
EDUCATION FOR
AFRICA

PURPOSEFUL EDUCATION FOR AFRICA

K. A. BUSIA

Routledge
Taylor & Francis Group
LONDON AND NEW YORK

BFI
BUSIA FOUNDATION INTERNATIONAL

Published in cooperation with
BFI in celebration of its silver anniversary

First published in 1964 by Mouton & Co.

This edition first published in 2023
by Routledge
4 Park Square, Milton Park, Abingdon, Oxon OX14 4RN

and by Routledge
605 Third Avenue, New York, NY 10158

*Routledge is an imprint of the Taylor & Francis Group, an
informa business*

British Library Cataloguing in Publication Data
A catalogue record for this book is available from the British
Library

ISBN: 978-1-032-32672-6 (Set)
ISBN: 978-1-032-35371-5 (Volume 2) (hbk)
ISBN: 978-1-032-35391-3 (Volume 2) (pbk)
ISBN: 978-1-003-32665-6 (Volume 2) (ebk)

DOI: 10.4324/9781003326656

Publisher's Note
The publisher has gone to great lengths to ensure the quality
of this reprint but points out that some imperfections in the
original copies may be apparent.

Disclaimer
The publisher has made every effort to trace copyright
holders and would welcome correspondence from those they
have been unable to trace.

New Introduction to the Reissue of 2023: Revisiting "Education for What?"

In the original introduction to this book, Professor Emery Ross quite rightly pointed out that Dr Kofi A. Busia had done something that few educators would approach because they felt it would be impossible, that is to write "briefly and simply about a philosophy of education for the huge diverse complex called Africa". He judged that Busia had succeeded because of his experience both inside and outside of Ghana and inside and outside of Africa.

Re-reading this book in preparation for writing this introduction, I cannot help but agree, and reflect on the sixty years that have gone by since we, as children, remember father working intensely on several projects at once, including this one. He would disappear from Holland to various places in Africa leaving mother waiting patiently for him to return, while we experienced what we considered a normal childhood. Only years later did we realize he was working on the three manuscripts that comprise this series (in addition to *Urban Churches in Britain, 1966*), while we were in exile. Thus, mother's waiting was always an anxious waiting for his safe return, and our childhood was far from normal. The research for this volume, is what enabled him to return to the continent and take care of the concerns of his party of exiles at the same time. Published in 1964, the first year after our arrival in England, it must have been in its final stages of preparation the six months we were in Mexico at the end of 1962.

It is interesting to reflect on the decisions father was making concerning our own education in those years. Moving to Europe had not been his first choice to spend his exile years, which were I believe, longer than he first anticipated. After his Fellowship years at the Institute of Social Studies in The Hague, and as Professor of Sociology and Culture of Africa at the University of Leiden (1959–1962) he could not return to Ghana. For the sake of our schooling he had hoped to return to an Anglophone country in Africa, but it was not a moment where those states felt they could entertain the man who was leader of the opposition to Kwame Nkrumah. He could have found refuge in several of the Francophone countries at the time, but because he wanted us to be able to fit seamlessly into the educational system whenever we returned to Ghana, he felt the differences in educational systems radical enough to raise us in England instead. His decision was based on the informed understanding he had gained while researching this very book. As it turns out, we attended the American School in The Hague (1959–1962) because the British school was full. This was followed by a semester of Summer School at the American School in Mexico, after which we were home schooled for six months in preparation for primary school in England. And sitting at the dining table tutoring his children, father was finalising this very book.

Still, "education" is such a vast, contested, mutable subject one would ask, why, with all the changes that have taken place over the last six decades, would we wish to republish this small book after all this time? The reasons are many: not only because we are doing it as part of a series of our father's publications about Africa to see the wisdom and foresight he had about the continent in those years, but also because, on reflection the administrative issues he tackled remain germane. The pedagogical and philosophical issues he faced remain with us, and thus the observations he made and the questions he raised, remain pertinent: the question of what is a purposeful education remains with us, as they remained with him throughout his life.

He opens the preface to the book "At the end of my first year at secondary school (Mfantsipim, Cape-Coast, Ghana), I went home to Wenchi for the Christmas vacation. I had not been home for four years, and on that visit, I became painfully aware of my isolation. I understood our community far less than the boys of my own age who had never been to school. I felt I did not belong to it as much as they did. It was a traumatic experience. My awareness of the problem of the relevance of education to society must have begun then." (p.7) This book is in fact a mapping of his recognition, in his own words, from that same preface, that "Over the years, as I went through college and university, I felt increasingly that the education I received taught me more and more about Europe, and less and less about my own society." (p.7)

Far from remaining alienated from his society[1] father goes on to explain how in fact the trauma of that experience led him to make the effort of comprehending and redressing that gap an urgent mission in his professional life. He engaged with that question constantly throughout his career. It was a gap experienced not by him alone, but also by his peers who walked that same path to schooling and higher education, and who thus supported him in the work that he did subsequently. For this research he spoke to heads of state and government as well to the heads of educational institutions, their faculty, staff, and students. The matter of the implications of that gap he had experienced, and thus fashioning an appropriate education to redress, was for my father and his peers a collective engagement, for on it rested the future of the continent.

Sixty years ago, our father set out with dedication to ask, "to what extent do the educational institutions of Africa meet needs and aspirations of the societies they seek to serve?"

(p.8) He attempted to answer that question by visiting a range of institutions over three years from 1960–1962. The book was based on research of various national patterns of education across the continent, including of the foreign, indigenous cultural, and recent nationalistic patterns extant in the countries he visited. He had as an objective, how to link the best from without, to the needs from within, to help us all grow. What indeed is a philosophy of education that can guide a continent facing rapid change; change in everything from the recognition and articulation of common concerns to the speed of communications. "I visited all types of schools, primary, vocational, secondary, and technical schools, farm institutes, adult education and rural training centres, teacher training colleges, museums and universities." (p.9) His wide range of institutions, including museums, was insightful. He saw much being done, rapid growth and change in structure and infrastructure, pedagogy, and administration, through the diversity of all kinds of educational establishments. He wanted to discuss the specific question of the ends of education because "everywhere education was expected to help fulfil national aspirations and goals."(p.9)

Given his experiences as a young man, father begins with a brief investigation in the first chapter into the foundations of "Traditional Education". To him, the essential goal of traditional education was admirable, and remains challenging: "The young were prepared for their social roles in the home, the village, or town, or tribe. They were constantly made aware of the community to which they belonged, in and for which they were trained through work and play and religious rite; through song and dance and folklore, through customary services received or given within the all-embracing network of family and kinship ties. This was training in citizenship." (p.16) Where citizenship could be defined clearly in small culturally cohesive contexts and where the emphasis of behaviour and on becoming was unmistakable. The goal of education was "to inculcate this sense of belonging, which was the highest value of the cultural system. The young were educated in and for the community's way of life." (p.17) The question, therefore facing the educational sociologist in 1962 was: what sort of people were being educated, to become what sort of citizens, in our increasingly complex societies? What indeed is the relevance of all of that past to us today? Education in contemporary Africa presents many complex problems, but in the search for ends, the modes of traditional education, then and now, point to a fundamental truth which cannot be ignored – What sort of men and women? What sort of citizens?

Within that context, the first issue that father faced was that when talking about educational policies in contemporary Africa we had to deal with the "Educational Policies of the Colonial Powers", a legacy that is still with us. Needless to say, there was little unifying them, the administration of education being as diverse as the forms of colonial administrative practice so to speak "from Cape to Cairo." What it seemed they did have in common, was a disregard for the needs and aspirations of Africans themselves, the colonies existing only in furtherance of the needs of the so-called homeland. "The various policies of the white rulers have left the new nations of Africa legacies of educational philosophies premised in varying degrees on European societies and on their racial or cultural superiority or both. These are philosophies which the new nations of Africa reject. The challenge facing them is that of preparing their nationals for the duties and responsibilities of citizenship in modern self-governing States, within the interdependent community of nations. They have to develop and implement educational policies in consonance with their new status and new aspirations, and in the context of the rapid social changes of Africa which have the pace and dimensions of a revolution." (p.28)

Thus, the issue that all African societies faced at the moment of independence, when they were seizing control of their own educational policies, was that the education they had inherited still seemed to separate them from the homes in which their students lived. Their schools did not seem to prepare their children for their own societies. It quickly becomes noticeably clear all over the continent that education policies and systems needed to be adapted to local conditions. Springing from that, there were questions to be faced that remain with us today – including for example the fundamental question of in which language are our children being schooled?

Those are the starting points for this slender book of a hundred pages. Within these pages father goes on to tackle, through a series of well-sequenced chapters: "The Search for Science and Culture" which is then placed in the context of "Education and Manpower Needs" and which then raises questions about "Education and Social and Civic Life" and therefore a discussion of "The Teacher and His Role". How do we train teachers to fulfil those roles and so it follows to ask what is "The Role of the University"? Having discussed all these questions, my father ends up finding his central final question, "Education, for What?"

I remember father always saying that for him, the heart of this book lay in that last chapter "Education, for What?" And that remains the central question that we face sixty years later. It remains the question that must guide us as we continue to face an ever increasingly changing world and make the policies that guide our education all over the continent, and indeed, the world. As I was preparing this introduction, I was invited to speak at the *World Conference on Education and Restitution* sponsored by The Association of African Universities (AAU), UNESCO, and the Pan African Heritage Museum, held at the AAU Headquarters in Accra (30 August–1 September 2022). The theme of the conference was "The Past, The Present, and the Future: Afrofuturism and Africa's Development". The conference was addressed by many distinguished Africans including H.E. Arikana Chihombori Quao, former AU Permanent Representative to the USA, Prof. Olusola Oyewole, (Secretary-General, AAU) Hon. Kojo Yankah, (Founder of the Pan African Heritage Museum) with a Keynote delivered by H.E. Abdoulrahamane Diallo (UNESCO Country Representative, Ghana). What all of these speakers charged the assembled university professors, administrators and students, to do was to provide positive outlooks on the future of education by looking at the past, with the purpose of regaining what we have lost and move into a great future by reconceptualizing and reclaiming African Arts, Culture, and Heritage.

We were collectively enjoined to develop strategies to promote excellence in the African higher education system and to begin by redefining the curriculum for teaching and learning in African universities and ensuring that our graduates possess the skills and competencies required for them to contribute to Africa's development. We were also encouraged to use our language, songs, music, thoughts, and other cultural forms to solve problems peculiar to us and all Afro-descendants. I couldn't help but bring to mind a line from the final chapter of this book: "Education must pass on the heritage of the past, cope with the present, and prepare for the future." (p.96) A line which summed up the philosophy undergirding the study. We are still asking the same questions, with the same objectives father had six decades ago. When I was asked to share my poetry at the opening session of the conference, having just re-read the book I felt inspired by its questions to write this invocation, with which I will end this introduction.

Who has what rights of kin?

In claiming the heritage of our past
Who do we say we are, what is that past?
From where do we amass this knowledge
we know we must gather to survive?

What is heritage and what an inheritance?
And how and with whom do we share it?

If national independence leads
To International interdependence
then what mean these legacies
Of borders, boundaries and boundedness?

In coping with this present
In what language, and how, do we speak?
If cultures are expressible in no language but their own
What mean these dreams of a common tongue?

When home and school pull apart
To whom are we obliged?
When school and work are not aligned
Where is the place we live?
What is the life we give?

To prepare for any future....

Abena P.A. Busia
Brasilia, October 2022

Notes

1. I was surprised to find this extraordinary charge made by Walter Rodney in *How Europe Underdeveloped Africa* (1974) who commented on reading it: "No wonder the professor became the alienated professor he became. Eventually, Busia knew so little about African society that he proposed that independent Africans should 'dialogue' with the fascist racist white minority that maintains apartheid in South Africa," completely missing the point of father's work and certainly not reading even the next paragraph of the book or anything father had ever published, though all his major works were readily available by 1974 when Rodney published his seminal volume. It seems to me Rodney was responding, as all worthy radical people did in those days, simply to the fact that father had been the leader of the opposition to Kwame Nkrumah back in 1957.

A Note on *K.A. Busia on Africa*:
An Anniversary Set

The idea for the establishment of the Busia Foundation was conceived of by Mrs. Naa Morkor Abrefa Busia (1924–2010) to honour and perpetuate the memory of her late husband Professor Kofi Abrefa Busia (1913–1978) and remind his communities of his ideas and ideals. Busia had an enthusiastic commitment to democracy as the "moral language" of all humanity and to equality of all persons. It has been observed that Busia's ideas have survived the radical populism of the 1960s, the militarism of the 1970s and the 1980s and emerged vindicated in the 1990s. It was to honour these ideas and ideals, and the way he tried to put them into practice over his short term of office as Prime Minister of the Second Republic that the Busia Foundation was established. The Busia Foundation was formally launched in July 1998 in commemoration of Busia's 85th birthday, with Busia Foundation International established three years later. Among the aims and objectives of the Foundations are to preserve and disseminate Busia's ideas and ideals widely by promoting and fostering his concerns for human rights, and the basic needs of people and civic education through a celebration of their vibrant culture. An anchoring task of this aspiration is to establish and maintain a library and resource center and to publish or assist in the publication of his books, little-known articles and unpublished papers, an aspiration started by the republication of the three books of this set.

Prof. Busia published five books in his lifetime, the first his revised doctoral dissertation *The Position of The Chief in The Modern Political System of Ashanti* (1951) remains today a classic, still in print seventy years after first being published. *Urban Churches in Britain: A Question of Relevance* (1966) is remarkable for being the first sociological study by an African scholar of the British rather than the other way around as it had been for centuries. Commissioned by The World Council of Churches as a part of his World Studies of churches in mission, though it is a model in its approach, and its critique of its subject courageously honest, it remains a study of its time and place. Busia's other three books that comprise this set, though also of their time and place, concern an Africa in the throes of dynamic change and retain a relevance that make them worthy of consideration that republication will bring.

The Challenge of Africa (1962), *A Purposeful Education for Africa* (1964) and *Africa in Search of Democracy* (1967) between them are a comprehensive view into Prof. Busia's concerns published in an incredibly productive five-year period. The three books are together a wonderful reflection of Prof. Busia's work and thinking about the rapidly changing Africa of his day. His was the Africa new to independence, undergoing a thorough going soul searching on how to create the institutions that will craft new complex nations out of old equally complex societies. They have proved prescient in their articulation of the issues we are still facing to establish security and stability for ourselves and control our own natural and human resources. Busia's commitment to understanding how to pass on the heritage of the past, to cope with the present, and prepare for the future remains a constant thread throughout these works, all of which raise questions that remain with us. In dedicating his life to establishing viable liberal democracies on the African continent where each person was "his brother's keeper" Busia showed his firm conviction that liberal democracies are not an invention of ancient

Greece, but a reformulation of traditional ideas of communal caring and governance by consensus, writ large on a more complicated sense of collectivity.

Busia Foundation International is pleased to present this set *K. A. Busia on Africa* bringing these seminal works together in commemoration of the 110th anniversary of his birth and in celebration of the establishment of the Foundation. The studies are published in their entirety, but each of them with new introductions. *Where A Purposeful Education for Africa* is given another introduction by the series editor his daughter H.E. Professor Abena P.A. Busia, we are pleased to present *The Challenge of Africa* and *Africa in Search of Democracy* with new introductions which are the works of Prof. Busia himself. The on-going process of organizing the Busia archives led to the discovery of two scarcely known public presentations by Busia which now serve as wonderful introductions in his own words to the concerns of those two books. Shortly after Busia became the first African Professor at the University of Ghana in 1954, he attended the School of Advanced International Studies of the Johns Hopkins University conference on "Contemporary Africa". The address he gave as the principal speaker at the closing banquet is published here for the first time as the new introduction to *The Challenge of Africa*. This talk, given eight years before the publication of that volume, reveals how early in his career he started grappling with the issues the book covers. A decade after that dinner-time address, Busia's reputation as a fighter for democracy was firmly established. That Prof. Busia, at the time leader of Ghana's opposition in exile, was honoured to be asked, by the society for individual freedom, to speak at Runnymede on 15 June 1965 in commemoration of the seven hundred and fiftieth anniversary of the signing of the Magna Carta, makes this clear. That address now serves as the introduction to *Africa in Search of Democracy*. We hope that the republication of these works, making his own words more readily accessible will encourage the serious study of his ideas which must be the basis on which his legacy is built.

Abena P.A. Busia
Brasilia, Brazil October 2022
For Busia Foundation International
Akosua G. Busia, President

PUBLICATIONS OF THE INSTITUTE OF SOCIAL STUDIES

SERIES MINOR
VOLUME IV

INTERNATIONAAL INSTITUUT
VOOR SOCIALE STUDIËN · 'S-GRAVENHAGE
1964

PURPOSEFUL EDUCATION FOR AFRICA

by

K. A. BUSIA

1964

MOUTON & CO.

LONDON · THE HAGUE · PARIS

Printed in The Netherlands.

INTRODUCTION

To write cogently and perceptively and at the same time
briefly and simply about a philosophy of education for the
huge, diverse complex called Africa: one feels that for not
a few educators this would approach the impossible. Yet
Dr. Kofi A Busia has done it. A perceptive African,
knowing both Africa and the West, has done it. This com-
bination of perception leading to knowledge, then to for-
mulation, then to action, opens many doors. And not only
book doors, but doors to all human understanding and
confidence and co-operation.

This book now published should be a stimulus to thought-
ful men and ·women concerned with the broadest and
deepest aspects of education in Africa and elsewhere on
our globe. It is written by an African who has seen much
of Africa outside his own Ghana; of other parts of the
world; of various national patterns of education; of the
foreign cultural and nationalistic patterns put down upon
Africa. He now seeks usefully to link the best from
without to the needs from within Africa, to help the very
best from within grow for the good of all – of all peoples
in all lands.

This is a philosophy which should nourish the life roots
of our more and more compacted world in this day of

unprecedented spread and speed of change, of communications, of common concerns.

This present contribution by Dr. Busia, coupled with many others he and colleagues of diverse backgrounds and experiences are making, should greatly help Africans and people of goodwill everywhere as they educate themselves and their children to use the constantly widening powers our Maker opens to us all.

EMORY ROSS

PREFACE

At the end of my first year at secondary school (Mfantsipim, Cape-Coast, Ghana), I went home to Wenchi for the Christmas vacation. I had not been home for four years, and on that visit, I became painfully aware of my isolation. I understood our community far less than the boys of my own age who had never been to school. I felt I did not belong to it as much as they did. It was a traumatic experience. My awareness of the problem of the relevance of education to society must have begun then.

Over the years, as I went through college and university, I felt increasingly that the education I received taught me more and more about Europe, and less and less about my own society.

That feeling became challenging when as Professor of Sociology I gave courses at the Institute of Education at the University College of Ghana on education and society. I found that my students, many of them trained and experienced schoolteachers or headmasters had experienced, like me, the unhappy gap between what was taught at school and the life and needs of our society. My lectures dealing with the problem excited unfailing interest year after year, and I felt challenged to write a book about it.

A new challenge came in December 1959, when I

Page 8, line 30
for Idenburgh *read* Idenburg

attended a Colloquium in Paris, organised by the International Social Science Council of Unesco. About thirty educators, sociologists, anthropologists, economists and administrators from different countries, Europe, Africa, Asia and America, were brought together to consider the problems of education in Africa.

We first met in one group, and put questions to one another from the different approaches of the disciplines we represented. Then we divided up into separate groups, according to the different disciplines, to study the questions, and met later as one group to consider the answers. The inter-disciplinary discussions were stimulating. It was during one of the sessions at this Colloquium that I felt I should embark on a research project dealing with the question: to what extent do the educational institutions of Africa meet the needs and aspirations of the societies they seek to serve?

I first discussed the idea with Mr. H. L. Elvin, Director of the Institute of Education, University of London. It was one of his edifying interpositions at the Colloquium that stimulated me to decide on the research project. The discussion I had with him encouraged me to pursue the matter further.

When I returned to Holland where I had just been appointed Professor of Sociology at the Institute of Social Studies at the Hague, and also to the newly established Chair of Sociology and Culture of Africa at the University of Leiden, I discussed my idea with the Director of the Institute of Social Studies, Professor E. de Vries, and with Mr. P. Idenburgh, Secretary of the Afrika Studiecentrum at Leiden. They both gave me warm encouragement. I am grateful to them, and to the respective Boards of my two Chairs, for allowing me to make some of my research trips to Africa during term time.

I am also grateful to Dr. Emory Ross and Dr. Wilton Dillon of the Phelps Stokes Fund, and Mr. M. Josselsen of the Congress for Cultural Freedom, whose warm encouragement and active support made it possible for me to obtain the necessary funds. In this regard, I wish also to thank Dr. Karl W. Bigelow of the Teachers' College, Columbia University, and Mr. Vernon Eagle, Executive Director of the New World Foundation. As a result of contacts and discussions arranged for me by Dr. Emory Ross, the New World Foundation made grants to me for my work through the Phelps-Stokes Fund, and Mr. M. Josselsen also secured funds from the Congress for Cultural Freedom for some of my trips to Africa.

During 1960, 1961 and 1962, I made ten trips to Africa from the Hague where I was based, covering Senegal, Liberia, Sierra Leone, Togo, Nigeria, Uganda and Kenya. I visited all types of schools, primary, vocational, secondary, and technical schools, farm institutes, adult education and rural training centres, teacher training colleges, museums, and universities. I saw much being done in the field of education: new buildings going up, curricula being revised, and facilities for vocational, technical, and professional training being rapidly expanded.

In this short book, I do not attempt to give a full report of my study, but only to discuss the specific question of the ends of education, because the massive and feverish expansion of educational facilities I saw during my tours convinced me that Africa was in search of a social philosophy of education. Everywhere education was expected to help fulfil national aspirations and goals.

9

My debt of thanks is a huge account. I was overwhelmed by the help and kindness I received wherever I went, from the heads of university colleges, and schools and their staffs, and from Ministries and Departments of Education. I wish to express my thanks generally to all who gave me hospitality, or arranged transport for me, or took me round to schools and colleges, or spared time to talk with me, or arranged group discussions for me.

I would like to thank also the heads of States, President L. Senghor of Senegal, President V. S. Tubman of Liberia, Sir Maurice Dorman, then Governor of Sierra Leone, the late Sir Milton Margai, then Prime Minister or Sierra Leone, the late President S. Olympio of Togo, Sir Abukakar Tafawa Balewa, Prime Minister of Nigeria, and Mr. S. Akintola, Premier of the Western Region, for the personal interest they took in my work, and the help they graciously gave me during my visits to their respective States.

Finally, my special thanks are due to Mr. K. Ampom Darkwa, my Research Assistant, who conscientiously, willingly, and efficiently shouldered burdens which made possible the production of this book.

Oxford, March 1964   K. A. Busia

TABLE OF CONTENTS

CONTENTS

I. TRADITIONAL EDUCATION

Traditional African education was directed towards ends which can be perceived by considering what was done. There were systems of education in Africa before the colonial period; for every community must have a way of passing on to the young its accumulated knowledge to enable them to play adult roles and so ensure the survival of their offspring, and the continuity of the community.

In African communities, the older generation passed on to the young the knowledge, the skills, the mode of behaviour and the beliefs they should have for playing their social roles in adult life.

The young were taught how to cope with their environment; how to farm, or hunt, or fish, or prepare food, or build a house, or run a home. They were taught the language and manners, and generally the culture of the community. The methods were informal, the young learnt by participating in activities alongside their elders. They learnt by listening, by watching, by doing. In many practical ways they learnt how to live as members of their community.

It was recognised that the way in which the young would fulfil the duties of their social roles would depend on the sort of persons they became. So they were taught the community's standards of conduct. They were taught how to speak, how to respond to greetings and how to behave towards members of their family and community as well as to strangers. Above all, they were taught their roles in the all-embracing network of kinship relations, and what their rights and obligations were within it. They were taught that their behaviour was a matter of concern for all their kinsfolk to whom how they behaved and what they did would bring honour or dishonour. In different ways and situations, the young learnt what the community regarded as good, and what it regarded as evil, and caught the community's concept of the good life. There were warnings to refrain from doing what the community judged to be evil, and encouragement to practise what was judged to be good. The emphasis on behaviour and on becoming was unmistakable.

Community life, even for a homogeneous tribal society, is complex. It must have unifying ideals. In traditional African societies this was provided by religion which pervaded all activities and all relationships. Education inculcated a religious attitude to life: reverence towards nature and the unknown universe.

The cosmologies were based on the existence of a Supreme Being who was Spirit and Creator, and the source of all power and energy. He granted existence to all created things. He animated the gods, the spirits and human beings, animals, rivers, trees, rocks and all matter. Their metaphysics conceived the Creator as a universal vital Force that animated and energized all created things whose real essence consisted not in matter but in the energy and power infused into them by the Creator.

The world above, the world around, and the world below were accepted and explained in terms often incom-

14

patible with modern scientific knowledge. There was much that was superstitious and unscientific in Africa's interpretation of the universe. There are extant notions about such phenomena as eclipses of the sun, or the moon, or shooting stars, echoes, the falling of rain, mineral substances, witches, death, and spirits which portray superstitions long shattered by scientific enquiry and discovery in other countries. This indicates one of the fundamental needs of the new education: the teaching of science, to substitute tested knowledge for superstitition.

This, however, lies in the future. Traditional education taught a world-view based on polytheistic religions which conceived a world of many gods and spirits. The peoples manifested through their religious rites, a strong sense of dependence on the Supreme Being, on deities and spirits, on the departed ancestors, and on local resources – earth, rivers, food.

It has been erroneously held that the traditional religions of Africa were not concerned with morality. Religion did give support to the laws and customs of each community, and to its accepted rules of conduct – courtesy, generosity, honesty, and identification with one's family and kindred. What is noteworthy, however, is that the morality sanctioned by religion enjoined good behaviour within the family, tribe or nation with which the deities or spirits were particularly associated. Selfcontained, isolated tribes conceived the activities of their gods to be limited to their own needs and aspirations. Principles of morality are universalized on the basis of the social experience of a people.

Everything the young were taught had relevance to the life and culture of the community and to the kind of life they were expected to lead. The goals of traditional systems of education were clear. The older generation imparted to the young the skills they needed for making a living. In their conditions, and with the available knowledge and technology, the skills to be learnt were few, and could be imparted through informal methods. Traditional Africa did not have open to it the different occupations and specializations that the introduction of European science and technology and the beginnings of industrialization have made available. In the new situation in contemporary Africa, training the young to earn their living is discussed in terms of facilities for producing technologists, scientists, engineers, doctors, economists, administrators, teachers, nurses, and many other specialists; but all this is basically an extension of the traditional concept of imparting to the young the skills necessary for coping with their environment.

In the traditional system of education the need to train for adult life was also clearly seen. The young were prepared for their social roles in the home, the village or town, or tribe. They were constantly made aware of the community to which they belonged, in and for which they were trained through work and play and religious rite; through song and dance and folklore, through customary services received or given within the all-embracing network of family and kinship ties. This was training in citizenship. The greatest concern was shown about the sort of persons the young would become, and the life they would lead as members of the community.

Though traditional Africa had many cultures, they all appear to have emphasized as a summum bonum, a social sensitivity which made one lose one's self in the group; the

16

kinsfolk were, and lived as members of one another. It was the goal of education to inculcate this sense of belonging, which was the highest value of the cultural system. The young were educated in and for the community's way of life.

Much of that way of life is passing. The solidarity of the small, homogenous group of kinsfolk, the close-knit organisation of the village, or chiefdom or tribe, the rituals by which their sense of belonging was constantly renewed, have all been undermined. Larger and more heterogeneous groups and societies have emerged. The social awareness that now needs to be inculcated in the young must include these larger groups; the concept of membership of one another must extend beyond the tribe; the attention to the individual's behaviour must not be limited to concern for his conformity to the established ways of the group, but must, in the contemporary situation, show a deeper respect and appreciation for freedom and change. But the essential goal of traditional education was admirable, and remains challenging. Traditional education sought to produce men and women who were not self-centered: who put the interest of the group above their personal interest: whose hearts were warm towards the members of their family and kinsfolk: who dutifully fulfilled obligations hallowed and approved by tradition, out of reverence for the ancestors and gods, and the unknown universe of spirits and forces, and a sense of dependence on them. There was always the awareness that human life was the greatest value, and increase in the number of the members of the community the greatest blessing the gods and spirits and supernatural powers could confer on the living.

Education in contemporary Africa presents many complex problems; but in the search for ends, traditional education points to a fundamental truth which cannot be ignored — What sort of men and women? What sort of citizens?

II. EDUCATIONAL POLICIES OF THE COLONIAL POWERS

Everywhere in Africa, there is evidence of the impact of colonialism. Under it, the old world of Africa has been changed, by the invasion of European science and technology, and new ideas and institutions, such as schooling. The school has been one of the factors of social change in Africa. This is most clearly seen when formal schooling is first introduced into an illiterate community. Consider, for example, the children who first go to school. They have to learn new ways. The whole rhythm of their life changes. They begin to live by the clock which regulates school life. They have to sleep and wake up, and wash or bath at times different from what they had been used to; often they begin to wear clothes or school uniforms different from the clothes they are used to wear at home; the times when they take their meals may have to change to fit in with school life; they are no longer able to work and play as before, with the other boys who do not go to school, for school hours impose limitations or compel a different routine; they are unable to share in mother's or father's work and learn at their side the activities which take place during the hours of school. At school, they get used to desks and tables, and reading and writing materials. They come to have new needs, such as a room and facilities for reading and writing. They make new demands on the home, and reciprocal adjustments constantly have to be made to accommodate the few who go to school.

There are not only changes in habits. Those who go to school learn new facts, and new ideas about such things as diseases, nature and natural events different from the bits of knowledge they have picked up at home. School and home seem to pull apart.

The longer the children stay at school, and the more they learn, the further apart home and school seem to pull. This is so because they learn more about countries and peoples in far away Europe than about the needs and problems of their home and kindred. The school does not seem to prepare the child for its own society.

What, then, were the policies which guided education under colonial rule? For an answer, we take a brief look at the policies of the colonial powers.

British educational policy has been stated at different times in various reports. The most comprehensive statement of objectives was made by the Advisory Committee on Native Education in the British Tropical African Dependencies in a memorandum presented by the Secretary of State for the Colonies in March 1925.[1] The objectives set out in the memorandum included the following: that education should be adapted to local conditions: that an important role should be assigned to religious training and moral instruction, which were stressed as being fundamental to the development of sound education; that local vernaculars should be taught, and text-books in these vernaculars should be prepared; that provision should be made for the training of an adequate number of teachers

[1] Cmd 2374.

20

on whom a sound system of education depended; that technical and vocational training was essential for development, and should be provided; that special importance should be attached to the training of girls, and that provision should be made for visiting teachers, for adequate supervision, and for a government system of inspection to ensure that good standards were attained and maintained. These objectives were reiterated in a number of subsequent reports, such as in a report published in 1949 by the Committee of African Education in Kenya,[2] the proceedings of a Conference on African education held in Cambridge in 1952, and published under the auspices of the Nuffield Foundation, or in the 1953 de Bunsen Committee on Education in Uganda and in a sessional paper subsequently issued by the Uganda government.[3]

There was little to quarrel with in the objectives as they were set out, but there was a wide gulf between what was stated and what was actually practised and achieved. In particular, there were two serious shortcomings. The first concerned the concept of the pace of change. Even when education was considered in relation to the avowed goal of selfgovernment for the colonies, its radical implications for territories soon to become independent were not sufficiently appreciated to arouse the sense of urgency the situation demanded. Consequently, a low priority was accorded to educational expansion which the imperial government tended to see in terms of consumption rather than investment. The second was the failure to see edu-

[2] *African Education in Kenya.* Report of Committee 1949. Para. 252, 253.
[3] *Education in Uganda* (= *Sesional Paper No. 2* of 1958/9), Para. 9 and 10.

cation realistically in terms of the needs of African society. The consequences of these shortcomings will be observed in the postcolonial period.

France does not appear to have had a uniform educational policy for her colonies prior to 1903. In a government school opened in St. Louis in 1816, a start was made to teach the Senegalese through the medium of their own Wolof language. But the first government school opened in 1887 in the Ivory Coast concentrated on the teaching of French. The main purpose was to train interpreters and clerks. Early policy in Madagascar, as officially stated in 1899, was to give the young Malagasy an education which would give them such skills in industry, commerce, and agriculture as were required by the French settlers in the Colony, for their mining, industrial and commercial establishments.[4] The vocational training for these services was given in the French language.

It was in 1903 that a general plan of education for all French African territories was drawn up. It embodied an educational policy which aimed at establishing French culture in Africa, based on the conviction that France had a civilizing mission in Africa – to introduce her colonial subjects to the culture of France. Accordingly, a uniform system of education was established in all French territories, so that whether an African child went to school in Senegal, Mali, Dahomey, Ivory Coast, Upper Niger, Equitorial Africa or Madagascar – in whichever part of the vast French African empire – he studied in a school system modelled in content and method on that of metropolitan France. There was little attempt to adapt methods or

[4] Article 5 of Ordinance of April 16, 1899.

curricula to the needs and conditions of individual territories. The philosophy underlying the education policy for French colonies was that of assimilation into French culture. That policy was pursued until 1944.

At the Brazzaville Conference of that year, it was recognized that some modifications should be made, and objectives believed to have taken account of the new social, political and economic facts of the dependent territories were formulated. These objectives included the teaching of a better way of life to the masses of the people; the selection and training of an elite to fill junior administrative posts in government; the teaching of the French language; the adaptation of primary school curricula to local needs; the development in each territory of secondary and technical schools which were to be the same in every way as similar institutions in France; and the selection of suitably qualified Africans to pursue higher academic and professional studies in France. This modified policy was, in fact, still dominated by the design to spread the French way of life, and to produce educated Africans who would be at home in French culture. It was still a cultural imperialism which African nationalism has challenged. The new States which have emerged from French colonial rule seek policies that take account of their cultures and aspirations.

Belgian policy was to build in the Belgian Colony of the Congo a modern State that would provide for the Belgian residents all the amenities that Western science and technology and knowledge could give. These benefits would also be gradually conferred on the Africans through a process of education which, as the Belgian rulers saw it, would develop by logical stages. Primary education and vocational and technical training were to be extended gradually to the whole population, before a start was made on secondary education; and when a sufficient number had received secondary education, then some could proceed to university education. Congolese schools, and educational institutions were to be identical with those of Belgium, so that diplomas and certificates earned in Congolese schools would be equivalent to those earned in Belgium. No questions of adaptation appeared to arise, for the aim was seen to be that of lifting the Congolese into what the rulers regarded unquestionably as the higher civilization of Belgium.

The Belgians were critical of policies like those of the British which gave secondary and even university education to a few when a large proportion of the population remained illiterate. They did not approve of sending Congolese to Belgium for higher education; "civilization" was to be brought to the Congo. They justified their policies on the grounds that they aimed at raising the whole people to a higher level, and not at bringing the benefits of civilisation to just a few who would become an elite.

The results of Belgian education policy are now well-known. When the Congo became independent in 1960, 64 per cent of the population was said to be literate; this was high for an African country. The facilities for technical education were also as good as could be found in any Colonial territory in Africa; but there were only 16 university graduates out of a population of more than 13 million, and none of them had served in positions in government or industry where responsible policy decisions were taken. The country was not prepared for the responsibilities of self-rule.

The Colonial educational policy of Portugal is part of the wider imperial policy of integrating her African colonies into metropolitan Portugal. Consequently, the schools are vehicles for introducing Africans to Portuguese language and culture, and to the Catholic religion which is the national religion of Portugal. After some five hundred years of Portuguese rule, only about 3.6 per cent of the present African population of Mozambique and Angola have sufficiently mastered Portuguese language and culture to qualify for acceptance as "assimilados", to enjoy full Portuguese citizenship. There are no institutions of higher learning in the territories. The aim is not to train Africans for self-government, but to educate the African population to become nationals of Portugal, speaking Portuguese, assimilated into Portuguese culture, and converted to the Catholic religion. The basis of the long cherished policy is being challenged. Africans are demanding the right to govern themselves, and to choose their own goals.

Spain, like Portugal, has premised her policy on what appears to be an indefinite perpetuation of colonialism. The policy being pursued in Spanish Guinea discourages the use of local vernaculars, and pays scant regard to African traditions. The schools are vehicles for assimilating the African population into Spanish culture and the Catholic religion; but at the pace Spain has moved, it will take centuries for the mass of the African population to qualify for political and cultural assimilation. In the meantime, Africans receive technical and agricultural training for their part in the economy. The minority that has qualified for assimilation has been placed in junior administrative and professional posts. The policy does not seem to anticipate self-government or the rise of African nationalism.

The knell of colonialism is ringing all over Africa, and the educational policies of Portugal and Spain are seen by other Africans as anachronisms.

The status of Africans in the Republic of South Africa justifies a review of South Africa's educational policy along with those of former colonial powers. An interdepartmental Committee on Native Education in what was then the Union of South Africa, 1935-6, noted that "the education of the white child prepares him for life in a dominant society, and the education of the black child for life in a subordinate society". Since 1948, the Nationalist Party has taken steps towards implementing its apartheid policy based on the philosophy of separation. It is based on the theory that Whites and Blacks are different races possessing different cultures, and that they must live apart in separate communities in order to give each race the best opportunity of living its own life, and realizing its own goals. The African should not be given an education that would raise expectations that cannot be fulfilled. It was the present Prime Minister, Dr. H. F. Verwoerd, who when he was Minister for Native Affairs stated that "there was no place in the European Community for Africans beyond the level of certain types of labour". Parts of his speech delivered in Parliament are worth quoting.

"What is the use of teaching the Bantu child mathematics when it cannot use it in practice? That is quite absurd . . . Education must train and teach people in accordance with their opportunities in life . . . Racial relations cannot improve if the wrong type of education is given to Natives . . . Above all, good racial relations cannot exist when the education is given under the control of people who create wrong expectations which clash with the possibilities in this country. It is therefore necessary that the Native education should be controlled in such a way that it should accord with the policy of the State."[5]

Accordingly, the Bantu Education Act of 1953 was to "prepare the natives more effectively for their future occupations". The implementation of the apartheid policy was carried further by the separate University Education Bill introduced in the South African Parliament in March 1957. As reported in Hansard of 27th to 29th May, 1957, the Minister of Education defended the bill by saying that it was a further step in the implementation of racial apartheid, or separate development, by providing for university institutions to suit the requirements of the different non-white groups of the population. These were to complete the educational structure already separately developed for them from the elementary school stage upwards. The government was firmly convinced that the leaders of the different racial groups could only be satisfactorily educated in racially homogeneous university institutions where they could participate fully in all activities in their own languages and cultural atmosphere.

The fact must be faced that the policy is designed not for equal, though separate development of the races, but for the assurance of permanent white domination. It has been justified on the ground that it promotes the cultural development of the non-white races in accordance with their own traditions within a Bantu social framework. It is a philosophy of education based on the "inherent aptitudes of native races", and on a fallacious doctrine of cultural hegemony. Africans have no inborn social or cultural traits

[5] Dr. H. F. Verwoerd, House of Assembly Debates (September 14–18, 1953), Vol. 83 Col. 3576.

that cannot be modified by learning. Cultures do not permanently divide races. They are learnt; education can bridge cultural gulfs.

The various policies of the white rulers have left the new nations of Africa legacies of educational philosophies premised in varying degrees on European societies and on their racial or cultural superiority or both. These are philosophies which the new nations of Africa reject. The challenge facing them is that of preparing their nationals for the duties and responsibilities of citizenship in modern self-governing States, within the interdependent community of nations. They have to develop and implement educational policies in consonance with their new status and new aspirations, and in the context of the rapid social changes of Africa which have the pace and dimensions of a revolution.

III. THE SEARCH FOR SCIENCE AND CULTURE

Men are educated in and for a given society. It is this that sets the tasks of an educational system. The invasion of European technology has changed the old world of Africa. It has introduced new ways of earning a living, and new skills and professions; work in the mine, the commercial city or harbour or the factory offers new opportunities; men have formed new associations to pursue new interests; the bicycle, the car, the train and the aeroplane have accelerated mobility; the school, the radio, the press and television have widened men's horizons. Possibilities not previously conceived have been revealed: that more babies can survive; and men and women's expectation of life can be extended beyond middle age; the earth can be made to yield more food for all to enjoy; more durable and comfortable houses can be built; water can be brought to the farm and distant home; men and women can be more mobile and travel long distances in much shorter time; they can communicate with one another beyond the limits of the human voice, and visible space, and the passing moment; new knowledge and skills can be gained; political rule can be effectively exercised over larger areas, and peace, order and co-operation maintained among different ethnic and racial groups. These revealed possibilities make Africa eager to apply available scientific techniques to the

29

solution of her problems – of food, housing, health, communication, education and government. She is striving to catch up with the rich and industrialized world.

The educational policies and systems inherited from the former colonial rulers have been found in one respect or another to be inadequate for the new tasks, and the fulfilment of the new aspirations. At what was then the Nigerian College of Arts, Science and Technology at Enugu, Eastern Nigeria, a senior member of the staff explained to me: "The education given is not suited to the country. What the pupils learn at school is not related to the home. Education must be built on what is. The deficiencies of the educational system appears here in the college. In the secondary schools, the students are crammed and spoonfed. When they come here, they cannnot relate problems to practical life". This pointed to a common deficiency; courses and examination systems encouraged mechanical memorization; what was learnt at school often had little relevance to the African environment. In Guinea, another criticism expressed was that education under French rule had been planned to provide opportunity for only a few to become an elite assimilated into French culture. In Uganda, it was the fact that too much attention had been paid to academic subjects, and too little to practical subjects which was singled out as the most flagrant failing; whereas in Morocco, it was the fact that the education had not been based on local tradition and needs and had therefore failed to bridge religious gulfs among Moslem, Jew, and Christian, and radical gulfs among Arab, Berber, and European that caused the most concern. In Dakar, criticism was implied in the new policy that education should aim at contributing with maximum efficiency to the economic and social progress of the country, and at the same time provide for the individual in his national environment. These and other criticisms showed that education was expected to undergird national unity, be related to African conditions, and meet the needs of an independent African State in a technological age.

Over and over again, criticisms were expressed especially about the failure of the former colonial powers in two fields of education which are of particular importance to present-day Africa: science and culture.

There was general recognition of the fact that Africa needed scientific knowledge for combating poverty, ignorance and disease. She needed it for entry into the modern world. But it was also clear that the search was not only for new scientific knowledge, but also for continuity with her past. There was an insistence on the study of the cultures of Africa. How, it may be asked, can this be reconciled with the fact that the educational problems of Africa must be tackled in the context of rapid social change, and that the more science and technology invade Africa, the greater the compulsion to change old ways.

The new states of Africa seek to rediscover and preserve their cultural heritage and history, neglected or contemned under colonial rule, not only as a foundation and an inspiring expression of their independence and nationhood, but also in order that they may make their own distinctive contribution to the common cultural heritage of mankind. There is therefore a general desire that education should be rooted in Africa's own cultural heritage and values, and have relevance to African societies.

It is a paradox of history that a nation's culture may undergo wave after wave of change through the acceptance of new inventions and ideas, or borrowing from other peoples' cultures, and still remain distinguishable and unique.

There is a sense in which science is international; but cultures remain distinguishable and peculiarly indigenous, despite the impact of science on society. In spite of contacts between peoples, and the borrowing of cultural items and patterns, a universal homogeneity of cultures has not emerged; because a people's past, and their own selections and adaptations give a unique character to their total culture, and this gives them a national identity and pride.

There is throughout Africa a desire for changes in the curricula of schools to enable pupils to enter more fully into their own local cultural heritage. The question of language teaching was often raised in this context.

Language is an integral part of culture. But language instruction in Africa poses problems, practical as well as theoretical. In the States of Africa which were formerly Colonies, the languages of the former metropolitan powers have been retained as the official as well as national languages. French or English, as the case may be, is often the only language through which members of the different tribes of a new State can communicate with one another. There are practical reasons for the retention of these European languages. African languages are numerous, and some of them have not yet even been reduced to writing. Linguists estimate that there are over eight hundred different languages spoken by the different ethnic communities of Africa. Hence European languages are retained as national languages because they make it possible for the different ethnic groups of a new State to communicate with one another; they are also the means of communication between Africans from different parts of the Continent, and between Africans and non-Africans. The European languages are international. They also have scientific, technical and literary works; they are therefore a more convenient media of communication.

Nevertheless, there is the proven fact that a child learns quickest through the mother-tongue which is also the best and closest link between school and home. Moreover, African cultures are rooted in African vernaculars. The oral traditions, the history of the drum, the rich imagery, the meaningful prayer, the lore of the priest, the soul-stirring dirge or song, are all given their fullest and inimitable expression in the vernaculars. To lose one's vernacular is to impoverish one's culture. The awareness that a people's culture cannot be fully expressed in any language except its own has aroused a new interest in African languages.

For example, Guinea has adopted a new policy, and a determined effort is being made for the three major languages spoken in the country to be taught in the schools in addition to French. In Tunisia, the long-term aim of the government is to use Arabic as the medium of instruction in all primary education. In Senegal, the stated official policy is that educational activity should lead as soon as possible to the general adoption of a common language and the sharing of a single culture by the various ethnic groups in the State. Morocco has similarly recognized the importance of developing a national language. All these aspirations underscored the crying need for more and more research on language learning, reform, and unification: and not only in language, but in all the various fields of culture – music, art, oral tradition and history; it is demanded by the national awakening in Africa.

33

The emphases on science and culture show the common awareness that a new social order is being created in Africa, and that schools and colleges are seen as instruments for preparing students for existing societies as well as for the social changes likely to occur in the immediate future as far as they can be foreseen. Educating for a new social order compels a consideration of ends. It is essential to have a sense of direction especially when so much is changing, and there is such a flood of new ideas, and so much uncertainty about old values and standards. On the one hand is the striving for progress through science, and on the other, for continuity and self-assurance through a country's own culture. There is need for a philosophy of education in which these and other goals are synthesised; social change sets various tasks for education. In the next chapter we discuss the problem of manpower.

IV. EDUCATION AND MANPOWER NEEDS

Many African States have embarked on development plans calculated to increase their standards of living. These plans aim at increasing productivity in agriculture, forestry products, animal husbandry, and minerals; at developing road, rail, water and air transport; at establishing secondary as well as heavy industry, and at increasing the volume of trade. Africa's industrial revolution has begun.

It has become increasingly clear that the development of human resources is as essential for economic growth as the development of natural resources. Throughout Africa, there are natural resources which are being wasted, or are unused because human talents have not been trained to exploit them. The crucial problem of Africa's economic development lies in the training of sufficient numbers of people who possess the specialised skills and competences necessary for building and operating a modern nation. Education has a part to play in economic growth.

Nigeria set up a Commission on Post-School Certificate and Higher Education which published its report in 1960 under the title *Investment in Education*. That title was a reminder that education is investment in people, and the report itself showed that a nation could expect the highest returns both individually, and socially, by investment in its human capital.

Due to the influence of that report and also to resolutions agreed upon at a Conference of African States on the Development of Education in Africa, jointly organised and convened by the Director-General of Unesco and the Executive Secretary of the United Nations Economic Commission for Africa, held in Addis Ababa (Ethiopia) from 15th to 25th May, 1961,[1] it is now becoming a part of the philosophy of education in contemporary Africa that education should be geared to manpower needs. It is right that it should be recognized that in a developing country, the consumer needs for manpower should be given prominence in educational programmes. It is easy to see why this should be so, and since there is a widespread need for manpower, the idea has been enthusiastically accepted by all African countries. It needs nevertheless to be said that it would be disastrous to plan education as though this were its sole purpose. That would lead to impoverishment. Productivity is not an end in itself, its value lies in the good life which it makes possible, and educators would agree that education should be concerned with the whole of life, and not merely with manpower needs; but they would also agree that, particularly in a developing country, education should be able to meet the manpower needs for rapid economic growth. This would have different implications for the different stages of education.

Education begins at birth in the home. This first stage of education has so little direct connection with the manpower needs of a nation that it is hardly given any

---

[1] *Conference of African States on the development of education in Africa. Outline of Plan for African Educational Development* (Unesco, 1961).

consideration when education is discussed in relation to the supply of manpower for economic development. Yet in Africa the new skills to be imparted at school are so different from traditional skills that the home background should receive attention in devising what is to be taught at school and how it is taught. It is because the home background has not been given the attention it deserves that the gap between school and home has been wide, and pupils have kept what they learnt at school separate from the lives they lived at home. We have already noted the criticism of a senior master at the Technological College at Enugu to the effect that students at the college were unable to apply what they were taught to the solution of practical problems. In fact, as he explained to me, the students were unable to see the connection between what they learnt from books and the practical problems of life around them. This has its roots in the methods that were used. Even if one were only concerned with manpower needs alone, the home and its culture should not be ignored. The State does not formally provide for the first stage of education which takes place before primary school begins at the age of six or so; but what happens then should have a bearing on what is taught at the other levels of education. The school should be seen as a link in the general process of education from the home through the various educational institutions to the larger society for which education seeks to prepare the young. For example, by the time an African child reaches primary school, he would have picked up much information about his social and natural world, much of which would be unscientific and even superstitious. Hitherto, formal education has left much of this uncorrected, and science teaching in particular has consequently failed to deal with wrong facts and beliefs learnt at home.

The next stage of education is the primary school which in most African countries begins at six. For most people in Africa formal education ends with the termination of the primary school cycle. From its early beginnings, the school in Africa has been mainly an avenue to white-collar jobs. Those who first acquired the rare skills of reading and writing found white-collar jobs awaiting them. This formed the pattern of expectations, and all who went to school set their eyes on white-collar jobs. Even those who had only primary school education could have their expectation for white-collar jobs fulfilled, because the rates of illiteracy were generally as high as 90 per cent or over. But the situation is now changing. Many African countries have rapidly expanded primary education during the last decade, and have turned out many school-leavers who are going about looking for employment as clerks. They flock to the towns looking for the jobs they have been led to expect. This is now a notable social problem all over Africa. The experience has led to a general criticism of primary school education as it was provided in the past; namely, that it did not pay sufficient attention to manual work. Past experience has taught that besides the basic skills associated with reading, writing and arithmetic, the primary school should prepare a pupil to train for an occupation. It should be given a practical bias. The point, it should be explained, is not that primary education should immediately contribute to productivity, but that it should inculcate respect for manual labour, and make pupils familiar with tools and concrete materials. In short, primary school education should develop in the pupils the attitudes and motivations demanded by modern technological society. This calls for changes in the content and methods of primary school education so that it can give the pupils an intelligent approach to the practical problems of home and community.

The skills required for achieving economic growth and raising standards of living are gained in post-primary institutions. It is post-primary education that increases the earning capacity of an individual. There are needy African students who are prepared to borrow money for secondary school and university education, because their enhanced earning capacity will enable them to repay the loan. There are poor families in Africa who borrow money or pool resources in order to give a member of their family the chance of post-primary education which the rest never had; they recognize it as a profitable investment. From the point of view of individuals as well as of governments money spent on education above the primary stage is investment in human capital.

It is at the post-primary level, but below the university stage, that the intermediate personnel so essential for economic development receives its training: the nurses, medical assistants, technicians, primary school teachers, agricultural assistants, foremen, laboratory workers, secretaries and the like. In all the new African States economic development is retarded by the dearth of technicians and other personnel required for the middle grades of industrial employment. Experience in some of these countries, for example in Nigeria and Ghana, has shown that it is possible to achieve high rates of economic growth, as much as 4 per cent per annum and over, with a small number of graduates and a level of illiteracy as high as

80 per cent, provided an adequate number of intermediate personnel is available. This means that the new States of Africa must give high priority to the establishment of secondary schools, and post-primary vocational and technical institutions for the training of the skilled intermediate personnel that a developing economy needs.

In fact, the proportion of skilled workers needed is so high that formal education at school cannot provide it fast enough, and systems of apprenticeships have to be devised to supplement the output of the post-primary institutions. This is also necessary to cope with the unemployment among primary school leavers. One of the primary schools I visited in Lome provided an illustration of the problem. The pupils at this school completed the primary school education at the age of 13 or 14. According to the headmaster's figures, about 10 per cent went on to secondary school. This was a comparatively high proportion; many schools in Africa do not attain to this, because the secondary schools are not available. The remaining 90 per cent constituted a problem. Under the conditions prevailing in Lome, the pupils could not begin apprenticeships until the age of 17, and the apprenticeships were a matter for private arrangements between the parents or guardians and the master craftsmen. Even where the pupils could be apprenticed, they would have 3 or 4 years of unemployment and enforced idleness between leaving school, and starting their apprenticeships. The fact was that many of them could neither find jobs nor apprenticeships. This situation, by no means unique, showed the need for instituting apprenticeships for trade training, as well as the provision of facilities for full-time and part-time courses at post-primary trade and technical schools. It is in this field that the failure of former colonial powers to prepare the colonies adequately for independence and industrialization is most glaring.

In every African country I visited during 1961 and 1962, there was evidence of the expansion or acceleration of technical and vocational education.

In Dakar, there were several secondary schools built since World War II, equipped for training in various trades - commercial, building and engineering. Liberia has had an expert from the United States to conduct a survey of her vocational education and to advise on its improvement and expansion. In the Ivory Coast, a separate Ministry of Technical Education had been set up in 1957 to give special attention to technical and vocational education. Two new vocational schools had been opened in 1959, bringing the total of such schools to five. Nigeria which already had well-established training centres at the Yaba Trade Centre, the Yaba Technical Institute, and three Regional Technical Colleges, had plans for more vocational and technical institutes. In October 1961, one of these, a new Technical College, had been opened at Ibadan to offer full-time courses in civil, mechanical, and electrical engineering. In Uganda, the Kampala Technical Institute was established in 1953 in order to step up the training of artisans and technicians in the technical, building and mechanical trades. In Kenya, a Native Industrial Training Depot started in 1924 had been taken over as an army training centre during the Second World War. When it was returned to the Education Department in 1949, it became the Kabete Technical and Trade School where a wide range of vocational and technical courses were given. Four other trade schools have since been established at

Thikai (1949), Sigalagala (1950), Kwale (1956) and Machakos (1958). A Charter to establish the Royal Technical College at Nairobi was issued by His Excellency the Governor of Kenya in 1951. By 1954, the College had started advanced courses in engineering and allied subjects. In January 1961 its work was supplemented by the new Kenya Polytechnic at Nairobi which offered courses in civil, mechanical and electrical engineering, science, commerce, and domestic science. According to their means, these African countries were increasing the facilities for training the technologists, technicians, and craftsmen that modern societies require.

The need for technically trained personnel in Africa is, however, unquestionably matched by the need for trained agricultural workers. More than 70 per cent of the working population of tropical Africa are engaged in farming, and agriculture provides African governments with the bulk of their revenue. Yet farming methods have remained wasteful, production low, and the conditions of living of farmers and their families at meagre subsistence levels.

The manpower needs in Africa for economic development must include a large proportion of trained farmers and agriculturists, for whose training more facilities should be provided, at all levels, in the educational system. Some African States have already learnt from experience that it is essential to increase agricultural productivity. They have found this to be a necessary foundation for industrialization and for economic growth; what has brought this home has been the fact that some African States have found themselves importing large quantities of food from foreign countries. This has been a drain on their foreign exchange, and a drag on the implementation of their development plans. So agriculture has come to be appreciated as the best foundation for security and prosperity, and the paucity of facilities for training for agricultural work as a serious deficiency.

Manpower needs both for industry and agriculture have emphasized the importance of secondary school education. An enquiry carried out by UNESCO into the educational needs of tropical Africa (1960-61) which covered 22 countries showed that the ratio of secondary to primary school enrolment was below 5 per cent in fourteen of the countries, between 5 and 7 per cent in four others, and above 7 per cent in the remaining four only. This lag in the provision of secondary education was serious, since the training of high-level manpower depends on the secondary schools.

But a fresh look at secondary education is called for. In most of the States in Africa, secondary school education has in the past been modelled on European or North American systems. In spite of this, some of the secondary schools have served Africa well; but oriented as they have been towards countries outside Africa, there has been an uneven bias towards literary subjects. A more serious criticism is that they have not given sufficient attention to the local problems and cultures of Africa. The students of secondary schools in Africa belong to the educated minority who must give leadership to their countries in all walks of life. Consequently, secondary education should be conceived not merely as providing training to meet manpower needs for increasing productivity, or only as an intermediate stage between primary school and higher education, but as general education which aims at producing young men and women for responsible citizenship in an

African community. The curriculum and content of secondary education should give the young people the knowledge they will require for discharging their responsibilities well. Having regard to this, secondary school curricula should get away from the literary bias and the early and narrow specialization in the upper forms which is the British model. At discussions I had in different African countries with secondary school teachers and headmasters, it was generally agreed that the curriculum of the secondary school should include the study of African conditions and cultures, and achieve a proper balance between the humanities, the social sciences, and the natural sciences, in a way which would enable the students to exercise an intelligent and constructive influence in society.

This is to be achieved without lowering standards. On the one hand, there is the need to maintain high standards, so as to ensure that secondary school leavers in Africa will gain admission to universities overseas; on the other, is the need for adaptations of curricula to the needs and realities of Africa at all stages in the educational systems. This thorny question has to be faced. When I discussed it in Dakar, for example, a senior Education Officer contended that "adaptation" could not proceed too far out of step, since the final school examinations were the same as in France. He thought some "adaptation" was possible: in the history syllabus, for example, world history could replace the history of France; or in geography, more attention could be paid to Africa; and "perhaps some adaptation in the natural sciences was possible" but there was a limit to what they could do. The real point, however, lies in seeing secondary education fulfil the purposes required of it in the context of the needs and aspirations of an independent African State. The answer seems to be the setting up of Regional Examinations Councils, similar to the West African Examinations Council which conducts examinations of standards comparable to those in Britain, but allows room for drastic changes in curriculum, if they are deemed to be necessary. The needs and aspirations of the society that an educational institution is to serve are basic factors for determining what should be taught, and the proportions and categories of the skills to be trained. These can be translated into the programme of the school or college only through continuous research and careful planning.

An educational system that seeks to meet manpower needs must be planned; for in the short-run, there can be an oversupply and consequent unemployment at any level of the educational ladder. As has been noted, the rapid expansion in primary schools has produced widespread unemployment among primary school-leavers. The economies have not expanded fast enough to provide them the jobs they expect, and they have not the skills for the available tasks that need to be done. In Ethiopia, emphasis on technical training resulted in the turning out of students for whom there was no suitable employment, because the economy did not expand quickly enough to absorb their new skills. In French West Africa, so much of the funds from FIDES (Fond d'Investissement Economique et Social) was invested in secondary education after World War II, that a lecturer of the University of Dakar expressed the view that "if secondary and primary education continue to grow according to the same proportion that we now have between the two, we shall finally have a structure not in the shape of a pyramid but of a column. This

45

situation will lead to the domination of completely uneducated masses by a highly educated minority which – and this is even more serious – would form a sort of caste, since those who would have been educated would possess means of educating their children to a far greater extent than the others."[2]

This points to another problem, that of achieving a balance in the structure of the educational system, both as to geographical distribution in a country, and the different levels, primary, secondary and higher institutions. This is necessary in order to avoid bottlenecks, overproduction, and unemployment. The skilled manpower turned out by an educational system should match current needs as well as demands in the foreseeable future, as far as these can be estimated. This calls for a Planning Authority to carry out surveys, assess needs, and plan to match demand and supply.

A balanced development of education cannot be attained at once. It has to be reached by stages. Priorities have to be decided in relation to available resources and needs. This demands continuous research, and co-operation among economists, educationists, and policy-makers. The desire to meet the manpower needs of a developing country has given educational planning in Africa a new dimension. The realistic planning of education as investment in a country's human capital requires manpower surveys to assess needs; the allocation of resources to the different phases of education – primary, secondary, technical, vocational, professional and adult; research to find out appropriate content for the curriculum, and the methods

[2] Assane Seck, "Education in French West Africa", *News Bulletin, Institute of International Education,* November 1960, pp. 52–54.

suited to each phase, and to the special needs of a country; and the fitting of all these into a country's overall development plan. This is what the new States of Africa must strive to achieve.

V. EDUCATION AND SOCIAL AND CIVIC LIFE

The social and economic development on which African countries have embarked is a social pursuit. It requires the co-operation of many people employing different skills and doing many different things.

In the last chapter, education was considered in relation to manpower needs. Educational planning in that context is an exercise in forecasting. It must be based on a vision of the country's total life as it will appear at the end of the period of the plan. The planners must have a clear picture of what they want. They cannot foresee every detail, but on the basis of the available data, they should consider their plan within the frame of the social order they seek to realize. It is an order to be achieved by all the citizens and for all of them in the life they share together.

This raises for Africa a special problem which no educational plan can ignore. It is estimated that there are one hundred million people in Africa who cannot read or write in any language. This is more than half the adult population. For the well-being of the community, provision should be made for this adult population to share in education. The children who are of school-going age are future producers; but the adult population must provide the labour force needed now.

Conditions in contemporary Africa show that the illiterate

adult population needs education, particularly in the three fields of health, agriculture and citizenship.

Health education is a fundamental need in Africa. There are few doctors. Some countries cannot provide even one doctor per 80,000 of the population. Infant mortality rises to as high as 700 per thousand in some of the new States. Many million hours of labour are lost annually through undernourishment, ill health, poor sanitary conditions, and inadequate medical care. The illiterate adult needs to be taught the basic facts of health so that he can look after himself and his dependants, and help to promote the health of the whole community. He needs to be informed about the nature of the more common diseases; about their prevalence, the way in which they are transmitted, and the methods of preventing or treating them. The elements of maternal and child care should be imparted to every potential mother. All should have some knowledge of general environmental sanitation regarding water and food and waste disposal. Sanitation is a way of life to be acquired by the child at school as well as the adult out of school. It is given expression in the clean home, the clean farm, the clean school or office, the clean village or town. The health of the citizen is needed for economic and social progress as well as for defence, and health education should be made an objective of adult education.

Health education gives opportunities which have so far not been seized to bring home and school closer together. If through the ignorance of parents the children at school are undernourished, or are provided with unbalanced meals at home, their performance at school is affected; they are unable to take full advantage of the opportunities offered them at school, and much of the teachers' efforts are wasted. The school has its own part to play too. An untidy classroom or unclean school compound or neglected school building does not provide a suitable environment in which to teach habits of cleanliness to school children. Children at school are given lessons in hygiene, but it is equally necessary to promote understanding and sound habits among parents and adults, and this must be one of the tasks of education.

Agriculture which is so vital for the economies of all African States is largely carried out by the adult citizens, many of whom are illiterate. They are still the backbone of economic life. But the old techniques handed down to them are no longer adequate. They are now required to produce more, to learn to use new tools, to improve the soil by new methods of drainage or fertilisation, or water supply and soil conservation, or grow new crops, or join others in co-operative farming and mechanisation. They are also expected to learn new methods in animal husbandry in order to produce more for a larger population. These are tasks for Adult education in the African context. Experience has shown that investment in practical forms of education to help the farmers achieves substantial increases in production.

An illiterate adult cannot take a full part in the social and civic life of contemporary Africa. With independence for his country that was until recently a colony, he has acquired the right to vote for members to local councils and national assemblies where the new rulers are chosen, and the laws are made; but his illiteracy disqualifies him from being a candidate for office. He requires information to help him understand the problems of the technical and social changes going on around him, or to discharge his new civic duties. So special programmes need to be devised to provide such information as part of adult education. African countries need a system of adult education inspired by a sense of urgency to provide training in effective citizenship for illiterate adults. Illiteracy is a temporary problem; it must be eradicated as quickly as possible; maximum productivity and social justice demand it.

It is not only the illiterate population that needs to be prepared for modern citizenship. During the last quarter of a century, the problem of adult education in Africa has been given attention by various governments, and by UNESCO. Programmes which have been launched have given different emphases, from literacy campaigns to community development projects. Some of the programmes have been designed to meet various needs of the literate section of the population also.

There are those who after completing their primary school education, return to live in largely illiterate communities where it is difficult for them to maintain the standards they had reached, let alone improve on them; there are others who did not complete primary or secondary schooling but desire to continue their studies; there are those who want vocational training outside the normal school system to improve their qualifications; or want to gain more understanding of the machinery of modern governments; or to learn more about other countries or international organisations like the United Nations and its organs, UNESCO, ILO, WHO, or FAO, and other bodies of that world organisation whose work now concerns all countries; or to understand contemporary economic and social problems of their own country as well as other countries; or to learn art, or music or literature. The different programmes of adult education operating in African countries seek to meet one or other of these varied demands. In the context of rapid social change in Africa, in which some of the things learnt ten or even five years ago are already out-of-date, and when the education received today may be inadequate to meet the needs of tomorrow, out of school adult education must become an increasingly important feature of the educational system.

Africa is in search of roots, for its dignity and self-respect. The desire to build on the best in the traditional culture is as strong as the desire for new knowledge and modernisation. Consequently, an important aspect of adult education has been the programmes dealing with African culture, with its music and oral tradition, drumming, dancing and traditional crafts. The cultural heritage continues to exert a powerful influence in the life of present-day communities. Adult education must concern itself more and more with a nation's cultural heritage because it expresses its way of life. It includes more than music, drumming, dancing, and traditional crafts. It includes moral codes and social sentiments, religious beliefs, and concepts of the universe and man's place in it. It defines social relations and obligations and duties. The peoples of Africa have experienced extensive and rapid social changes over the past century. They have accepted new techniques, new products, institutions and ideas; but their cultures provide needed social cohesion, and a foundation for continuity as well as change.

Many examples could be given to illustrate the projects of adult education in Africa. The scope has been wide and varied. Adult education has been recognized as a means of helping individuals and groups to discharge better their local, national, or international responsibilities. Its institutions have included Social Welfare and Community Departments, Rural Training Centres, District Farm Institutes, Youth and Voluntary Organisations, Vocational Training Schools, Residential Colleges, and University Extra-Mural Departments. Its programmes have covered self-help development schemes, youth activities, and national literacy campaigns. Its methods have included residential courses, seminars, one-day schools, lectures, discussions and correspondence courses; and its media have included press, film, radio and television.

One example on an impressive scale was the campaign of adult education launched by Morocco. It aimed at providing for young people between the ages of 6 and 14, and for adults who had had no formal schooling. It was estimated that there were more than one million in the first category – youth who had had no schooling. A special education plan was devised, extending up to 1967, to provide regular instructions of twenty hours a week for four years. The youth were divided into separate age groups for instruction. This plan is cited because it rightly conceived adult education as a full-time activity rather than an irregular, part-time one. That approach showed a sense of urgency and a realistic appreciation of the problem.

The needs of the adults were to be met by national literacy campaigns, the first of which was launched from April to June 1956, under the patronage of the late King of Morocco, His Majesty Mohammed V; provision was also made for courses to be given in civics, hygiene, animal husbandry, housekeeping, food preparation and manual crafts and arts in the towns and at rural centres. It will require sustained and very energetic efforts in the next few years if the goals set for the grand concept are to be realised by 1967. It deserves attention because it was a bold and imaginative enterprise.

Projects for adult education started in the Ivory Coast since independence may also be cited in illustration, because it was a field which was neglected in former French territories. Centres have been established to teach adults to read and write. Several of the centres were established specially for women, and besides reading and writing, lessons were given in child care, housekeeping and sewing. In 1959, a National Service for Rural Education was formed, and mass education teams of primary school leavers were trained to launch community development projects which included the teaching of modern agricultural techniques to farmers. Political leaders appealed to their party members who were literate to regard it a civic duty to help their illiterate fellow-citizens. Through lack of personnel and sustained enthusiasm, these efforts did not produce staggering results, but they marked an appreciation of the problem and a desire to cope with it.

Two training centres in East Africa may be cited as examples of projects set up to meet the needs of literate adults. One is the Jeannes School in Kiambu, near Nairobi in Kenya which was started in 1926 as a rural development centre. It was taken over by the Kenya Government in 1949, and at the time of my visit in 1961, the work of the school was in three sections: first, was the preparation of young Africans for works in various government departments, or in African District Councils; second, courses for older people who were already established as farmers, shopkeepers, or civil servants to give them a better knowledge of their particular jobs and wider knowledge of the affairs of the country generally; and thirdly, special courses for women in agriculture, child care, cooking, hygiene, needlework, or how to run literacy campaigns. The records showed that the school had trained assistants for work in community development, health, probation, and co-operation; as well as rehabilitation officers, farmers, traders and librarians. Courses had also been given in African music and Swahili.

The other centre is the Nsamizi Training Centre at Entebbe, started in 1954 by Sir Andrew Cohen when he was Governor of Uganda. It was started as a local Government Training Centre, but it developed into a multi-purpose adult training centre. Residential courses were given at the Centre for administrative officers for the Provincial Administration; for men and women Community Development Assistants for the Ministry of Social Development; for Probation and Welfare Staff; Local Government Staff; and for Officers holding judicial and magisterial posts under African Authorities. There were also citizenship courses for senior officials of African Authorities, chiefs, council members, government officers, school teachers, clergy, and leaders of voluntary organizations. Special courses on "Modern living" were provided for women. These included child care, home management, cookery, nutrition, dressmaking, entertaining and budgetry.

In East as well as in West Africa, leaders in both education and politics spoke about the need to provide more facilities to enable women to play a new role in society. It was generally recognized that women had important roles to play as wives and mothers in the home, and as citizens in social and civic life; and that training facilities should be provided for them to enable them to participate more effectively in all spheres of life. Statistics compiled by Unesco in 1961 showed that the number of girls in primary schools was under 30 per cent of the total primary school enrolment, and only 22 per cent of secondary school enrolment were girls. So it was not only in adult education that more facilities needed to be provided for women, but in primary and secondary schools also. There was need not only to expand education facilities but also to improve, indeed, to reform the education for women and girls. There are traditional obstacles, religious, cultural, or economic to be overcome. Examples of the expansion of facilities during the last decade and substantial increases in the enrolment of girls at school, at all levels, could be cited from many African countries, from Ghana, Nigeria, Senegal, Sierra Leone, Uganda, or Ethiopia to illustrate the varying efforts being made to cope with the problem. The Ethiopian experiment may be given because it has an additional interest in that it has elicited international co-operation. The education of women was long neglected in that country; but in 1957, a new educational programme for women was inaugurated. New Centres for women's education were established, three of them in Addis Ababa, where courses were given in home economics, child care, and cottage industries. With the co-operation of United Nations organizations, principally FAO and UNICEF, the government provided for the training of teachers for home economics at secondary level. The projects resulted in increases in the numbers of girls enrolled at school at all levels from primary school to university.

The reform of girls' education advocated has called for emphasis on teaching girls new crafts to enable them to earn a living; so practical courses are now available in all

56

types of schools, primary, vocational, secondary and college, as well as in private homes and businesses. One example where an attempt was made to give practical training at a high level may be cited: The School of Home Economics which was started in Monrovia, Liberia, in 1949, and was incorporated with the University of Liberia in 1951. The school was set up to train young women in certain home arts and crafts in order that they might become better housewives, or acquire skills for earning a living. The courses offered included dressmaking, millinery, embroidery, crochetting, knitting, rug making, machine embroidery, and pattern drafting. It is a moot point whether a school of this type should be part of a university; a visiting commission has advised that the school should not form part of the university; but the fact that it was made a part of it shows the importance that was attached to this kind of practical education for women.

Nowhere in the countries I visited was what was being done for women considered to be enough, whether in the field of adult education, or in the formal institutions of school and college, for women's education had lagged behind that of men for generations; but it was generally accepted that there was an urgent need of the greater contribution that women could make to national life – in the home, and in social and civic life, in science and art, and in industry and commerce.

Education for social and civic life must teach the citizens not only new skills but also new ways of behaviour. Individuals must learn to live and work with others to achieve objectives which they all desire to attain. There must be a sense of belonging. For the multi-racial communities of East, Central and South Africa this poses a

57

crucial problem of citizenship. With regard to education, it was clear that harmonious social and civic life could not be effectively promoted through segregative racial educational institutions. In Uganda, where primary education was organized on a racial basis, and separate schools were provided for African, Asian, Goan and European children, the Government had in 1957 announced a new policy based on the principle of inter-racial schools. At the secondary schools, colleges, and the university where the medium of instruction is English, integration has been comparatively easy; but differences of language, background, diet and customs made it more difficult in primary schools. It is, however, proceeding, and there are African children in schools that were formerly exclusively European or Asian. Education is seen as an instrument for creating a harmonious community.

The existence of racial schools contributed to the bitterness that marked race relations in Kenya, and also to inefficiency, for small schools were maintained for separate racial groups where larger ones could be more efficiently and economically run. The policy of independent Kenya that all schools should be open to all races as has been the practice in institutions of higher learning expresses the conviction that education should help inter-racial understanding and co-operation, and the building of harmonious community life.

Besides a sense of belonging together, a community must have accepted standards of conduct for its public life. It is a commonplace remark that Africa is today a world of shaken beliefs and uncertain values. One of the most serious problems of Africa lies in the field of public morality. Some corruption may be found in the government and public services of most countries; but if selfishness and corruption go beyond a certain limit, they become obstacles to economic development and political stability, and threaten the State's well-being. Such a threat has become real and serious in some African States, and in several, public commissions have exposed corruption on a very disturbing scale. The States of Africa, engaged as they are in nation building must face the problems of corruption. The tasks of raising standards of living and of achieving a new social unity and cohesion can only succeed if the citizens share a common set of values, and standards of public morality which are supported by law as well as public opinion. To bridge gaps between literate and illiterate members of a community, or between school and home; to achieve harmony among different ethnic or racial groups; to have active and responsible citizens who work together for the common good, there must be clear values and definite standards of public morality and probity. Education for social and civic life cannot ignore or bypass this. Recent events in Africa have shown this to be an undisputably important need. What Aristotle once said of the city States of his day remains basically and challengingly true: "The State comes into existence for the sake of life; it exists for the sake of the good life". A State must have a conception of the "good life" and impart it to its citizens. It cannot thrive on shaken beliefs and uncertain values, or on widespread corruption in its public life. Training in citizenship requires an awareness of this problem. It is a narrow and inadequate concept of development to see it only in terms of roads, buildings and material structures. The quality of the nation, of its services, its culture, its life, depends on the quality of its citizens;

on the sort of men and women they are. This truth is expressed by a Ghanaian musician, Mr. E. Amu, in a popular song which has a refrain that may be translated:

> Whether the nation will fare well or ill,
> It is an old, old truth,
> That it depends on the conduct of the citizens.

Thus we are again reminded of the basic problem of education – the human capital; this time, in the context of public morality and citizenship. There was little sign of an awakening to treat this very real danger of widespread corruption as an educational problem. Yet plenty of evidence has been afforded of the injustice, inefficiency, waste of public resources, discouragement of foreign investments, the mistrust of government and government retaliatory oppressive measures, and the consequent political instability attributable to it.[1] Where a literate government rules a country whose population is largely illiterate, the occasions for disharmony and for corruption are many; the prospects are worse when a country undertakes to expand educational facilities without giving conscious consideration to the kind of person the educational system is designed to produce: it may be busy wrecking instead of building a nation. Education for social and civic life must pay attention to character, as well as production skills.

[1] "A Theory of Corruption", *The Sociological Review,* Vol. 9 No. 2 (July 1962), pp. 182–3.

VI. THE TEACHER AND HIS ROLE

A general shortage of trained teachers for existing schools; a telling exodus of trained teachers from teaching into other jobs; an insufficient number of candidates with the required academic standards coming forward for training; an inadequate number of teacher training colleges, and a shortage of training college staff, combined with rapid growth and accelerated programmes of massive expansion in educational facilities have created for many African countries a state of emergency in teacher-training which requires drastic measures and new methods of training.

All the African States have plans for expanding educational facilities, the success of which ultimately depends on the supply of trained teachers. It is the quality of the teaching in school which arouses the interest and fires the imagination of pupils and inspires them to choose their fields of study. It is the good teacher who touches off the spark that may burn into a steady flame.

Yet, in a good many African States, I found that because of the rapid expansion in schools, a heavy reliance was placed on teachers who were either untrained or had had inadequate training, and in primary schools, there were more untrained teachers than trained. Uganda was unique among the African States I visited in 1961-2 in having turned out more primary school teachers from the primary teacher-training colleges than could be employed; but the shortage of trained teachers for secondary schools was general, and it seemed that for a long time to come some of the African States would have to rely on expatriate staff for their secondary schools. The schools could not otherwise be properly staffed. In certain fields, notably in languages, science, and mathematics and in technical, vocational and agricultural education, the shortage of qualified teachers was acute.

The problem of providing teachers for the large number or new schools that were needed was made more difficult, because many trained teachers were leaving the teaching profession to go on to jobs that were better paid and had higher prestige. Independence and the jobs available in politics and the public services had altered the prestige of the teaching profession. The drift, had in some States, notably in Nigeria[1] and Kenya,[2] been on a scale large enough to cause concern.

The new African countries have to take a fresh look at the status of the teacher in the community, as well as his remuneration. The salaries of teachers have, on the whole, tended to lag behind the salaries of other employees of comparable educational attainments. The situation should be remedied by offering inducements in cash awards as well as in enhancing the prestige of the profession, in order to attract people of the right calibre and character. As it was aptly put in a Uganda sessional paper, "The boundaries of true educational advance are fixed, not only by the schemes that can be evolved and the finance that can be made available, but equally - and in the long run, more

[1] *Investment in Education*, p. 7.
[2] *Kenya. Report of Teachers' Salaries Commission*, p. 18, para. 59.

certainly by young men and women of the right personal qualities, and in sufficient numbers, offering themselves as candidates for the teaching profession."[3]

Teachers are needed on a large scale and quickly. This has called for an examination of the methods of training them. Teacher training in the past has generally been given in small residential colleges. The courses have varied in duration in different countries averaging one year for university graduates, two years for secondary school leavers, and three to four years for primary school leavers. This system has proved inadequate, not only in terms of the numbers of teachers trained, but, in some instances, in terms of quality also. Few countries have instituted a proper system of in-service training to enable teachers to learn new methods or adapt to changing social situations; a teacher who trained ten or twenty years ago may continue to teach in the way he was taught at school, or was taught when he was at the teacher-training college, unaware of new techniques, materials, or texts. In a rapidly changing society this is wholly unsatisfactory. Some African countries have leaped centuries in a decade. A teacher who never saw a radio or aeroplane until he was thirty or even forty years old, may, in the same town where he grew up, have to cope with a child who has always seen a radio at home, and has never known a world without the aeroplane. The teacher in such a situation has to be helped to rethink and adjust his methods.

A change of principle is discernible in the measures which some of the States of Africa have taken to deal with the emergency situation in teacher-training with which they

[3] *Education in Uganda (= Sessional Paper No. 2 of 1958/9).*

are faced; it is a change from reliance on comparatively long periods of initial training in the residential training colleges to shorter periods of residential training, combined with systematic, supervised in-service training.

The policy of short periods of initial professional training combined with systematic in-service training has evolved from the need to recruit large numbers of teachers during a period of large-scale expansion, particularly for primary schools. In many African States large numbers of young men and women who have had only seven or eight years of primary school education have been recruited and employed as teachers, after short periods of professional training varying from two months to a year. It is this that has necessitated the institution of in-service training, and the provision for adequate supervision, designed to prevent the standard and quality of education in primary schools from falling disastrously.

In Morocco, for example, nearly 13,000 were recruited as teachers in 1956 and 1957 alone. The recruits were given only three months' professional training, but in the course of their work as teachers, they were required to attend classes one day a week for further training, and they were supervised by school inspectors. Ten new regional teacher-training colleges were opened between 1955 and 1957; the period of professional training was cut down from nine months to five, in order to double the output of teachers from the colleges. University graduates were given three months' training, and secondary school leavers one year's training. At the same time, the number of school inspectors was increased to ensure that an inspector would not have to supervise more than 200 teachers. The inspectors observed lesssons given by the teachers under their supervision, offered suggestions for improvement, and gave demonstration lessons themselves. These measures were justified on the ground that they enabled the government to meet immediate demands for rapid expansion.

Other countries have taken similar measures. Senegal was introducing new reforms at the time of my visit. Teachers had formerly been trained only at the Sebikotane Teacher-training college, a residential college, providing a four-year course of training. The students were prepared for the secondary school leaving examination in the first three years, and the professional training was given in the fourth year. When I visited the school in May 1961, I learnt from the Principal that the majority of the students left at the end of their third year at the school, after they had passed the secondary school leaving examination, to go to Dakar University rather than stay the fourth year for the professional teacher-training course. The few who remained to complete the course could not even meet the needs of existing schools, let alone the new primary schools the government was building.

The government therefore adopted a new policy; this was to build regional teacher-training centres where selected primary school leavers were given an initial professional training lasting one year. Even this could not meet the need for new teachers, and other recruits from the primary schools were given short courses of training during school vacations. Provision was made for the work of teachers trained at the regional training centres to be supervised by "Principals". These "Principals" were recruited from those who had passed the lower level secondary school certificate examination (BEPC), and then given three years' general education and professional training simultaneously. This shortened the four-year course given at Sebikotane.

The in-service training systems which have been instituted in the different African States have served three different purposes. One kind of in-service training was designed to help those teachers who had started teaching without any training at all, or only a short preliminary training, in some cases lasting no more than three months. The in-service training devised for such teachers was meant to help them improve their knowledge of subject matter, as well as their skills in teaching, and in the use of equipment and text books.

A second kind of in-service training was to provide for experienced teachers who were selected to give supervision and advice to less experienced teachers who had had no training, or only short periods of training, or to enable experienced teachers who had been some time out of college to deal with new situations and keep abreast with the times. In order to relate education to the environment, and the needs and aspirations of African communities, curricula must be revised, and greater use made of new materials, and the new media of communication available. This type of in-service training is therefore designed to make older teachers familiar with new materials and techniques so that they are brought up-to-date.

The third kind of in-service training establishes it as a policy of regular training for teachers at all levels, covering the whole period of their careers as teachers. Some have advocated built-in credits to be earned at appropriate stages when a teacher satisfies prescribed requirements.

The situation of rapid social change calls not only for

additional facilities for training teachers, but also for improvements in methods. Steps have to be taken so that the adoption of shorter periods of initial professional training and new systems of in-service training are not accompanied by lowering of standards, but also by increasing efficiency. In several countries, shorter periods of training had resulted in a lowering of standards. So much has to be put into the short period of initial professional training that it is necessary to experiment with new methods, and to embark on an enterprising use of available media of communication, such as the cinema, radio, television, record-player, tape-recorder, teaching machines and other technological devices. The use of such media, and continuous research in their use for teaching and learning have to become regular features of teacher training programmes.

The special needs of Africa demand special attention for the training of teachers for secondary schools. The shortage of secondary school staff is acute. The problem is not only that of increasing facilities for the training of more secondary school teachers, but also of devising improved methods so as to cut down the period required for training them.

Plans of expansion and reform which were in progress when I visited Dakar exemplified new approaches to the training of teachers for secondary schools. In French-speaking Africa, the secondary schools were staffed mainly by expatriate teachers from France. In order to supply locally trained staff, an Institut de Préparation au Second Degré (IPES) was started at the University of Dakar to prepare holders of the baccalaureat, the secondary school leaving certificate, for secondary school teaching by giving them a two- year course of training: one year of general education, and one year of professional education. This preceded the new Higher Pedagogical Centre which, it is hoped, will serve other West African countries as well. The staff had already started research on curricula and methods best suited to Senegal, and to Africa generally. Owing to the general demand that education should be related more to the African environment than was the case in the past, this research was regarded as an important part of the work of the Centre.

In the Commonwealth countries of Africa, the problem of reducing the time for training secondary school teachers has been tackled by the introduction of courses leading to the Bachelor of Arts or Science degree in education. Teachers for secondary schools used to be trained at Institutes of Education attached to universities; university graduates were given a year's professional training at these Institutes. Since degree courses took at least three years, it meant that a secondary school teacher required four years of post-secondary preparation. In Nigeria, at Nsukka and Ibadan, and in East Africa, at Makerere, this is to be reduced by the establishment of three-year degree courses in Education in which professional training is given simultaneously with a general education appropriate for the secondary school teacher.

There are other needs which also call for new approaches. Additional facilities and new methods are required for the training of teachers for agriculture, and home economics, both of which are of special importance in relation to the African situation.

As has been apparent from the preceding pages, the contemporary situation of Africa demands fundamental and far-reaching reforms in education: revision and improvement of curricula, teaching methods, and the content of education at all levels. Though the content of education and methods of instruction are matters which are best left to teachers and professional educators, it is appropriate to consider in broad terms what teachers are expected to teach, having regard to the demands and aspirations of the African societies for which their students are to be educated.

We have already referred to the fact that for the majority of those who go to school in Africa, formal education ends with the primary school; and for most of the comparatively few who are able to go to secondary school, secondary education is not sought as a preparation to the university, but as the final stage of their formal education. This means that curriculum reform at the primary and secondary levels should aim at the difficult and dual objectives of making each stage an introduction to the next, as well as an end in itself.

The criticisms and complaints made in the different African countries I visited about their educational systems indicated the broad outlines of the changes required, and the general principles and concepts which should guide curriculum revision.

There is the unanimous agreement which we have already encountered, that all who go to school should be taught more about their own culture and social heritage than has been done in the past. Subjects like history, geography, civics, and the natural sciences should be more closely related to the African experience and background. New syllabuses should be devised to provide for the study of African history, art, music, sculpture, languages and oral

69

traditions to a much greater extent than has hitherto been done. Curricula, generally, should take greater account of the social relations and problems of particular African societies. The world of Africa, rather than of Europe, should be the focus of educational programmes for Africa.

But it is also generally accepted that Africa is no longer an isolated continent, and that educational programmes should therefore not only show an awareness of the world of Africa, but also of the wider world of which it is a part. Syllabuses in history, or geography or citizenship should give students an understanding of the life and social conditions of neighbouring African countries, and of the inter-relations and inter-dependence of the nations of the wider world.

We have also pointed out that all African countries place emphasis on technical education. This reflects the need for the study of science and technology. All students, from the primary school leaver to the university graduate, should be introduced at least to the outlines of the natural world as science has revealed it, and to the inventions and artifacts which technology has brought into homes, villages and towns in Africa, and into international relations. Moreover, all should have an education that enables them to understand the thoughts, attitudes and methods of a scientific and technological age.

There is a general concensus that education should prepare students for citizenship in an independent State. This requires curricula and methods which will develop the students' critical faculties, and enable them to decide intelligently on the social, political, economic and moral issues which they will have to face as citizens; and since citizenship is an art of living together with others, and is concerned with bearing responsibilities and co-operating to realize shared interests and desired goals, education must give a clear concept of values, and of good and evil. This implies activity directed towards the practice of the good life.

The points stated above indicate the changes required. It is for the professional associations of teachers and educators of different countries to determine and advise on the details of the subjects to be taught at the different levels of their educational programmes, in order to satisfy the needs and aspirations of their respective countries. Certain general points regarding specific subjects or stages may, however, be mentioned, in the light of discussions I had with teachers and educators in the various African States.

At the primary level, where education aimed at giving a general education, and imparting the basic skills of reading, writing, and arithmetic, rather than training for a specific vocation, criticisms of past systems and practices suggest that new curricula should be devised to give pupils training of the hand as well as of the mind. Instead of the former methods which emphasised passive receptiveness and memorizing, the hand and the mind should be partners in creative activity. Opportunities should be sought and provided, in the teaching of such subjects as handicrafts, nature study, geography and citizenship, for direct observation and manual activities, and for stimulating an intelligent approach to the practical problems of the home, the local community, and the nation. Since primary education is the end of formal education for many of the pupils, it should train them in healthy habits, give them an elementary knowledge of the human body and how it works, and of the bases of good nutrition and public sanitation and health. Primary education should help the pupils to cope with the environment in a rational way. Attention should be paid to the two disciplines which have been emphasised as being of special importance for Africa: agriculture and science.

Pupils, particularly those in rural areas, should be taught to have a sensible practical approach to farming, an understanding of its role in the economy, its techniques and problems, and they should have experience in the use of farming implements in order to appreciate the needs for further improvement in farming practice.

With regard to science, by the end of primary schooling, the pupils should have had enough scientific knowledge to dispel traditional myths and notions about the universe. They should have elementary knowledge of the scale of the universe, the size and rotation of the earth, the formation of clouds and rain, various forms of inanimate as well as living things, of matter and energy, and of the dependence of living things on sun, air and water; and some skill in operating simple machines, and an intelligent appreciation of the kind of thinking which lies behind their operation. Primary education should inculcate a scientific attitude. This is one of the crucial needs of Africa. It is in this sphere that some of the burning conflicts between tradition and change call for attention.

Primary education should also include training in citizenship, through direct observation and activity in the community; for citizenship is a life to be lived; it is learnt more by practice than by theory. It also involves moral values; education for citizenship involves training in behaviour. It has a social purpose.

72

The multiplicity of ethnic groups speaking many different languages makes research in language teaching and learning an essential task in the training colleges. As we have already stated, there is need for research in new methods, in the use of radio, master tape models, discs and playback equipment, and other media of communication.

We have already discussed some aspects of secondary school education in a previous chapter (IV). Another topic on which there were discussions was whether day schools or boarding schools should be preferred. Many teachers preferred boarding schools, in spite of greater costs, on educational as well as social grounds. The discipline of a corporate life in a boarding school was considered to offer the best opportunities for both character and intellectual training. In Dakar, for example, I was told by several education officers and headmistresses that the major problem of secondary education for girls was finding money for boarding schools, because parents, especially Moslem parents, insisted on boarding schools for their daughters.

Boarding schools gave other opportunities for influencing Community life. One of Dakar's leading secondary schools which I visited, the Lycee van Vollenhoven, had a boarding section with a well-equipped kitchen headed by a highly qualified French Chef under whose supervision balanced meals of African as well as French dishes were served. A criticism of the school, I was told, was that the students were fed too well. The reply of the school authorities to this criticism was that they were teaching the students the right diet for the future. The importance of this aspect of boarding school education is best seen in the context of malnutrition in Africa, much of which is due not so much to lack of food as to faulty dietary habits and ignorance of food values. A Joint Consultation Committee on Nigerian Education added another point in favour of boarding schools, namely, that in the context of the social conditions of Nigeria and other emergent States of Africa, secondary boarding schools met the needs of the community better; this was particularly so in the case of schools serving rural areas. The same was said of schools in Kenya which had to be residential in order to meet the needs of scattered rural communities.

The needs that primary and secondary schools are expected to meet dictate what those who are being trained as teachers for these institutions should themselves be taught in the training colleges. Besides the subjects which are normally taught in primary and secondary schools, and professional subjects like the history or theory of education, or the psychology of learning, or pedagogic methods, it emerged clearly from the discussions I had and the wishes generally expressed about the teaching of Africa that the social sciences (especially the sociology and culture of Africa) should have a place in the curricula of teacher training colleges. The demand for courses on African society and culture calls for the production of suitable text books and teachers' handbooks. Some of these will have to be written by teachers, or provided through the collaboration of teachers, training colleges and textbook producers and authors.

The fundamental quest is for a close connexion between what is taught at school and the kind of life the children are likely to live as adults; it is for the realization and the practical expression in education that school and community belong to each other. The success of teachers in this task depends on effective co-operation between parents, pupils, administrative officers and school authorities. In particular, on the effectiveness of the co-operation between home and school, between parents and teachers. Parent-teacher associations are needed in Africa as elsewhere; in those countries where these have already been started, as in Togo, they have given teachers and parents opportunities for explaining their problems and objectives to one another, and also a better chance of helping the young with whose training and welfare they are concerned. Above all, the relationship helps to make the school less of a foreign institution. Many parents are in a position to help the teachers the better to understand the African cultural heritage.

The obvious function of teacher training colleges is to train teachers: to teach the students the professional techniques they require for imparting knowledge and skills effectively to others. But it is clear that this is not all that the community expects of the teacher. The more important and significant function of a teacher training college is that of educating teachers as human personalities to help the development of other human personalities. It is this that gives unity to the school curriculum. The subjects of the curriculum should be designed to meet the needs of body, mind, and spirit, and the teacher must himself be aware of their relatedness. Teaching young people the elementary principles of health and the use and control of their bodies; or about their local community, and giving them experience of practical service to it; or teaching them to read or to acquire new manual skills in the use of pencil, pen, brush or tool, or training them in a vocation or profession to earn a living; or imparting to them scientific knowledge of the world around them; or teaching them moral values and the practice of religion, should all be seen as parts of a whole; that whole being the drawing out, the education of a human being. The adequacy or otherwise of teacher training must be judged in relation to this important role of the teacher. The teacher should be a good person as well as a good technician or specialist in the art of teaching; in fact, it is upon his quality as a person that the quality of education, and indeed of the nation depends. His pupils will look up to him; he must be worth growing up to. It follows that the teacher must himself have a clear idea of the sort of human beings his pupils should become. He must have a clear philosophy of education and of life.

The general interest in education in Africa, and the importance attached to it stem from expectations that it will produce effective, responsible citizens. Education for responsible citizenship and independence requires more than technical competence. It must have moral foundations, and promote integrity, co-operativeness, and social justice. Whenever a teacher stands before a class, besides the knowledge which he is able to impart with trained skill and efficiency, another process goes on: the life that his pupils or students catch from him. There is always the interaction of personalities, and the impact he has on his students.

In many countries in Africa, the teacher has served the community not only in the school, but also outside it. He is usually the backbone of voluntary organisations, and social services; leading choirs, boy scouts or girl guides, Red Cross activities, Peoples' Educational Associations, local government, and in many humanitarian activities.

Apart from these services, the teacher's role in the school is of vital importance for Africa. It is on his work that economic growth as well as political stability depends. He lays the foundation of national progress. A nation that does not show proper appreciation of its teachers or encourage public respect for them faces a serious threat to its standards and quality of life. We have already observed that African governments need to pay serious attention to the status of the teacher and to the public attitude to him. Every teacher, from the humble one in the remote village doing his work in obscurity, to the world-renowed university professor in the full glare of publicity, through his professional contact with his pupils or students lives on in other lives, a link in an unbroken chain whereby mankind is united through its cultural heritage that accumulates from age to age, passed on from one generation to the next by the teachers of each succeeding generation. The quintessence of every country's culture is what is expressed in its values of truth, beauty, goodness, and in active human sympathy. A teacher whose foremost task it is to transmit this must himself have a clear conception of it. He is "a high priest in the temple that has been consecrated to the glory and progress of humanity".[4] The teacher's role lays great and solemn responsibilities on him. Society and government have yet to give adequate practical expression of their recognition of that role.

[4] *Education and Society. Pakistan Committee for Cultural Freedom.* Inaugural address by A.K. Brohi, p. 3.

VII. THE ROLE OF THE UNIVERSITY

The skills required for modernising African societies, and for increasing their wealth are predominantly those that are acquired in institutions of higher learning. Universities and University Colleges have therefore mushroomed in Africa since the second World War.

The older universities of North Africa, in the United Arab Republic and Morocco, retain in their organisation curricula, and administrative structure, the impress of the Mediterranean and Islamic cultures from which they sprang; the newer universities, on the other hand, bear the stamp of the European Colonial powers which sponsored or established them. The universities of Africa, whether new or old, are rooted in alien cultures. This determines one of the major tasks for those concerned with higher education in Africa.

The dimensions of the problem, so far as the former British Colonies are concerned, can be seen from a study of the various reports dealing with the development of higher education in Britisch Colonies published between 1936 and 1954. Amongst them were reports on higher education in East Africa (1937), the Gold Coast (1939), Sierra Leone (1939) and the Report of the Commission on Higher Education in the Colonies (1945). The last report set out the principles and methods which guided the

78

British Government in the development of universities and institutions of higher education in the Colonies.[1] The most relevant of the Commission's recommendations were as follows: The Commission recommended that whenever an area could provide an adequate number of suitably qualified students, a university college should be established for it. Such colleges should be residential, open to both men and women, and should provide facilities for teaching and research in a wide range of subjects in the arts and sciences. They should also establish extra-mural departments to extend university education to members of the community outside their walls. The Commission emphasized that the colleges should be staffed with highly qualified and experienced people, and that provision should be made for the members of the staff to maintain contacts with academic institutions in Europe and other parts of the world. It also recommended the creation of an Inter-University Council for Higher Education in the Colonies, representing universities in the United Kingdom, and university colleges in the Colonies, to advise the Secretary of State on the development and academic policies of institutions of higher education in the Colonies. Other important recommendations were that the universities or university colleges should be autonomous like those in Britain, and should have similar constitutions and administrative structures: a Council, the supreme governing body and trustee of college property; a Senate to deal with purely academic matters, a Chancellor or Visitor whose duties are mainly ceremonial, and a Vice- Chancellor or Principal to head the administration of the university or university

[1] *Report of Commission on Higher Education in the Colonies*, Cmd. 6647 (London, H.M.S.O., 1945).

college. To ensure the achievement and maintenance of high standards, and universal recognition of their degrees, it was recommended that the colleges should, in the early stages, enter into special relations with London University, under which their students would be awarded London University degrees. These and the other recommendations detailed in the Report set the pattern of the universities and university colleges of British territories in Africa. The development of university colleges for Ghana at Legon, Accra, for Nigeria at Ibadan, for Uganda at Makerere, Kampala, and later for Rhodesia and Nyasaland in Salisbury, all followed the pattern recommended by the Commission. All these colleges entered into special relationship with London University, and their curricula and constitutional and administrative arrangements and procedures were modelled on British Universities, as were those of Fourah Bay College, Freetown, Sierra Leone, which, on becoming the University College of Sierra Leone followed its earlier connections and entered into special relationship with the University of Durham.

As regards Makerere, a Working Party sponsored in 1958 by the Secretary of State for the Colonies, on behalf of the East African Governments, to survey the future needs of higher education in East Africa recommended the establishment of a University of East Africa with constituent colleges located in the three mainland territories of Uganda, Kenya, and Tanganyika. This has since been implemented, and Makerere has become a member of an inter-State university, with the Royal College in Nairobi, and the third constituent college in Dar-es-Salaam.

Another African university which was based on British traditions was the University of Khartoum in the Sudan.

The Khartoum University Act of 1956 provided it with a constitution under which it set up administrative organs similar to those in British universities, and enjoyed a similar autonomy. But on the grounds that the students and staff had become embroiled in politics, the government of Sudan amended the University Act in 1961. The object and the effect of the amendments were the curtailment of the autonomy of the university. The appointments of the Vice-Chancellor and the Council of the University were vested in the President of the Republic, to whom the Council became merely an advisory body. All statutes proposed by the Council were subject to review and approval by the Attorney-General. The Act did not affect the curricula of the University, but the alterations in its administrative structure and in the powers of the Council removed cherished provisions of the British system, and significantly modified the role which it could play as a university. A similar repudiation of university autonomy has occurred in Ghana where the President in 1962 and again in 1964, arbitrarily dismissed senior members of the university staff.

Other traditions besides the British have been followed by new universities in Africa. The University of Liberia, established by Statutes passed in 1951 draws its inspiration from America, and is modelled on American traditions. The most notable aspect of its programme, in view of the new trends in university education in Africa is that the university, as officially stated in its prospectus, "is committed to the principle that there are certain kinds of educational experience which should be the common possession of all university students regardless of their vocational goals. The university, therefore, through the course prescribed for the freshmen (first) and sophomore (second) years, aims to strengthen and enrich specialized training by supporting it with a broad foundation of general education. This kind of education adds new dimensions to the life of the technically trained specialist and helps him appreciate the relationship of his life and work to the needs of society as a whole." This expresses what universities in Africa regard as a desirable goal to pursue, as discussed later in this chapter.

Another university inspired by American traditions is the University of Nigeria founded at Nsukka in the Eastern Region of Nigeria, in 1960. The model for the University of Nigeria is the American Land-grant College. It seeks to provide an education which is vocational and is also related to the social conditions and needs of Nigeria.

The two universities of the Congo Republic bring us back to European influences. The University at Lovenium, near Leopoldville, and the State University at Elizabethville follow the curricula af Belgian universities; the diplomas they award are designed to be equivalent in every way to those awarded by Belgian universities. Some special courses are provided in specific African contexts, such as African history, law, art, or languages; but this does not alter the essentially Belgian structure of the two universities.

The University of Dakar provides an example of yet another European pattern, that of France. It started as an Institute of Higher Studies in 1950, and subsequently became the University of Dakar. Although it is claimed in the University Calendar that its curricula are designed primarily to serve "the aspirations and needs of African peoples" and to "give the modern African an opportunity to examine the values of his own cultural heritage, and to acquire a deeper knowledge of other technical and moral values from the West", it was established as the eighteenth French University, within the centralised system of the universities of metropolitan France, and still retains the same structure, curricula, examinations and standards as other French universities.

Some of the problems to be considered regarding the role of the universities of Africa derive from the different traditions and patterns, Arabic, European, and American, on which they have been modelled. Three of these problems are general, and concern all the universities.

First, in the context of rapid social change, and the desire to raise standards of living, the curricula of the universities are expected to be closely adapted to occupational demands. A common criticism levelled against the institutions of higher education in Africa was that they had not done enough about teaching and research in technology which Africa so urgently needed, and a crucial question for universities in Africa is to decide what place to give to technology in their teaching and research programmes.

Some authorities think that technology should be taught elsewhere than in a university. In Ghana, and in Nigeria where the university colleges followed the traditions of the older British universities, it was left to Institutes or Colleges of Technology to provide technical education. In Ghana, a College of Technology was established in Kumasi to provide technical education and train the intermediate personnel that a developing economy needed. The scheme ran into difficulties. Both staff and students soon showed that they wanted to do degree work. They wanted the college to have the status of a university; the staff wanted this, because lecturers with the qualifications and experience required for the teaching, and especially the research, that needed to be done, could not otherwise be attracted, and the students wanted it for the status and brighter occupational prospects that a degree offered. The Kumasi College of Technology has been constituted a University of Science and Technology; and in Nigeria, it has been decided that the Regional Colleges of Technology established in each of the three regions should become Constituent Colleges of Regional Universities. These developments show that universities in Africa must have different structures and emphases. They may have to give priority to such fields as engineering, architecture, mining, or medicine, despite the greater cost involved; and consequently their structures will be different from those of the European universities on which they have been modelled. But a different structure need not mean a lowering of standards. The high standards which special relationships with European universities have helped to set are desirable and should be maintained. What Africa is crying for are competent technologists, and they are produced by institutions which maintain high standards.

The second topic of general concern is that concerning the provision of broad courses of studies at the universities, as against too early specialisation. It is felt that the students who qualify for entry into universities have generally a poor grounding in general education, and that they should not be encouraged to start specialist courses before this serious defect has been remedied. An even more cogent reason is that Africa needs university trained people with a broad background of general education which will help them to cope with the responsibilities of leadership which fall upon them. Students who graduate from universities in Africa have open to them positions which carry heavy responsibilities at a comparatively early stage of their careers. The pace of change is likely to be faster still in the future, and broad courses of study afford a better preparation for coping with it. The serious results of too early specialization which are deplored are the narrowness of outlook, and the gap which it creates between the specialist in the sciences, and the specialist in the arts, so that they do not understand each other's language and modes of thought. It is desirable that the scientist should have knowledge of the methods and approach of the arts, and that the specialists in the arts should have some training in the scientific method and approach. The leaders of a society which has to cope with the problems of rapid social change, such as African societies are having to do, must have flexibility and adaptability of mind and attitudes, and an appreciation of the variety of values. These qualities should be inculcated by a broad background of general education. The universities in Africa are beginning to provide broad courses of study in the first years of university education before specialisation begins. The programmes of Liberia University cited above is an example of this trend.

The third area of general concern is the recurrent theme that the universities and university colleges of Africa have not in the past given the study of African cultures its proper place and emphasis. There are innovations designed to provide courses in African studies which all students are expected to take.

Reforms in university courses which have been proposed

are intended to correct the three defects outlined above: first the failure to take adequate steps to prepare Africa to become the kind of technological society towards which, like the industrial countries of Europe, she desires to move; secondly, too early specialisation and the resultant bifurcation of the arts and sciences, and thirdly, the neglect of the study of the societies and cultures of Africa.

Though there is general agreement that the universities of Africa should pay greater attention to the study of Africa, I found different approaches and views on how this task was to be carried out.

There are those who consider that African studies should be at the core of the curricula of universities. In order to achieve this, they advocate the setting up of Institutes of African Studies to co-ordinate research, and advance the knowledge of Africa as an inter-disciplinary venture, covering the work of all the different departments, in the arts, the social sciences, and the natural sciences. This is the approach favoured by English-speaking Africa, where Institutes of African Studies are being set up in the universities at Accra, Ibadan, Ife and Freetown.

There is a different approach in French-speaking Africa, discernible in the provisions made at the University of Dakar where different institutes have been established for special study and research in different fields of African studies. There are, the Institut Français d'Afrique Noire (IFAN) which is a research institute of African ethnology; the Institut d'Etudes Administratives Africaines which trains local government officers; the Institut des Sciences Economiques et Commerciales Appliqués which studies problems of economic development; the Institut d'Etudes, concerned with Arabic studies; the Institut d'Etudes Pédagogiques concerned with education and teacher training; the Institut de Pédiatrie Sociale, and an office of the Institut de Sciences Humaines Appliqués in the field of the social sciences. This approach is one which seeks to provide for the study of subjects specifically concerned with Africa through specialised Institutes. The main body of degree courses, apart from minor modifications, corresponds with those offered in French universities. It was explained to me when I visited the university that the existence of the institutes did not mean that the Departments and Faculties were concerned with European subject matter only, but that, on the contrary, all the Departments and Faculties took an active interest in Africana. The Department of English, for example, was developing the study of African literature in English. The Institutes were meant to provide for the training of personnel needed for special services, such as local government and teaching, and to meet the needs of students who specialised in subjects that were no part of the normal curriculum of studies, as, for example, Islamic studies. Senegal, however, is predominantly Moslem, and the establishment of the Islamic Institute gives the clearest evidence of the approach being followed: minor modifications in the content of main degree courses and provision for African studies in Institutes on the wings of the University.

A third approach is provided by the universities of the Congo. Though it was contended that all teaching and research done in a university in Africa, whether in the humanities or the sciences, should be concerned with Africa, I found the system maintained was that of Belgian universities; but in order to meet specific needs, courses having special reference to the African environment were provided. At the State University in Elizabethville, for example, courses were given in linguistics with special reference to African languages, and in African history, art, tribal law, the economy of the Congo, and in physical and social anthropology with special emphasis on Africa. This approach is one of making adjustments in curricula in the humanities and sciences, but the content and structure remained modelled on Belgian universities.

Despite the insistence on African studies, there is an awareness that this should not destroy the supra-national outlook that makes a university a member of an international community of learning. There is a reaching out for closer inter-university co-operation, on the Continent of Africa, as well as outside the Continent. Hitherto, there has been little co-operation among universities in Africa itself; but at an international seminar on Inter-University Co-operation in West Africa held in Freetown, Sierra Leone in December 1961, under the sponsorship of the University College of Sierra Leone and the Congress for Cultural Freedom, it was agreed to form an Association of West African Universities as "a means of promoting closer contact and interchange of information and experience among West African universities and their members". The Constitution of the Association allows for the possibility of other universities of Africa joining. The recommendations suggested exchanges of staff and students; inter-regional co-operation in such fields as medicine, agriculture and forestry; the promotion of African studies; the study and teaching of English and French, and the languages of West Africa; co-operation in the production of books and periodicals, and the dissemination and exchange of information. Though academic people agree that such co-operation is desirable, its promotion involves political decisions. At the time I visited the University of Dakar, there were empty places which, as a senior professor explained to me, had been caused by the withdrawal of students from the Ivory Coast, "due to rivalry". The authorities of the Ivory Coast decided to start a university of their own. Subsequently, students of Mali and Guinea were also withdrawn; the professor commented "sharing facilities is easier said than done. Political considerations may hinder". Nevertheless, there is a new drive for inter-university co-operation in Africa. At the same time, the universities in Africa seek to maintain their contacts with European universities.

The Universities of the Republic of South Africa are unfortunately out of this drive for inter-university co-operation in Africa, because the apartheid policy as it has been applied in the field of education does not fit into the generally agreed principles of university education. The South African Governments policy of separate universities for the Bantu and European races appears to be premised on the philosophy that it is within closed societies that the fullest development is possible, namely, that it is within the separated homogeneous groups of European and Bantu that each racial group can advance its university education in the best and most desirable way. But the generally accepted view of universities conceives them as places where study and intellectual discussion are not limited to homogeneous racial groups, but where, without barriers of race, the pursuit of knowledge, or the search for truth is an adventure in which men and women of all races may join, and in the course of it, add to the ever-increasing heritage which belongs to all mankind. To erect racial barriers in university education is really to limit the academic freedom of universities. It will eventually lead to the impoverishment of learning, and to the failure of the universities to fulfil their functions properly, or attain acceptable international standards.

This brings us to an essential requirement of a university: academic freedom, without which it cannot fulfil its functions properly. A university must serve the country which supports it; but it must also gain acceptance as a member of the international community of universities. It must attain standards which will make the degrees and diplomas it offers internationally recognised, and its graduates acceptable in other universities and centres of learning; it should have a highly qualified and able staff which will be respected as colleagues by university teachers and professors elsewhere. A university should have the freedom necessary for it to fulfil its national and international responsibilities.

In Africa, the question of the academic freedom of the universities is a burning issue; in most instances, the universities depend entirely on government grants, and this makes it tempting for governments to try to limit the academic freedom of the universities or demand subservience to official views and policies; yet, unless a university had the freedom to control the admission, teaching, and examination of students; the appoinment, promotion, and tenure of office of its academic staff; the curricula and standards of its courses; the allocation of the funds at its disposal to different categories of its own budget; the determination of the balance it thinks it best to observe as between teaching and research, and the shape of its development, it could not discharge its function properly. Academic freedom is to be understood as guaranteeing at least the scope specified above.

Samuel Eliot Morison's plea for academic freedom in the context of America is equally applicable to Africa. He wrote: "We firmly believe that academic freedom is in the public interest. We do not claim it as a special privilege for our own protection; we uphold it for the protection of society, against the results of quenching the flame of original thought, the terrorisation of opinion, the subservience to authority which have been proved to be the bane or the destruction of every government that has adopted such procedures as their policy."[2]

The ultimate objective of a university is the production of a certain quality of man, and a certain quality of social life. The quality of social life a university seeks to promote is one based on democracy, inherent in which is the right and responsibility of every individual citizen to express judgment on local as well as national issues. It is in the public interest that a university should produce educated citizens who can exercise this discriminative function of judging issues soundly and responsibly. To do so, there must be freedom of access to different ideas, and of discussion and expression, not limited by racial barriers, or official demands of subservience, or terrorisation.

Universities in Africa, like other universities all over the world, are expected to contribute to the advancement of knowledge through research. As communities of scholars engaged on research, they must have the conditions of free enquiry favourable for new discoveries. In particular, they

[2] Samuel Eliot Morison, "Harvard University and Academic Freedom", *American Association of University Professors Bulletin*, Spring 1954.

are expected to advance knowledge of Africa, by focussing their research and teaching on the social conditions and environment, and the needs and aspirations of Africa. In all fields of study, in the natural and social sciences, philosophy and religion, history, geography and languages, there is still much to be learnt about Africa.

The universities of Africa are also expected to disseminate knowledge to the students within their walls, and through extra-mural activities to others outside their walls. Emphasis has been laid on the need for flexibility and for experimentation in instituting curricula and courses more relevant to the needs of Africa; and particularly, in providing courses on the cultures of Africa for all students, whatever their special fields of study may be. This cultural basis is considered essential for the understanding of their own societies, and for the recognition of the dignity and genius of the African; as well as of human dignity and genius generally, for the cultures of Africa must be seen and taught in the context of the cultural heritage of mankind.

A primary function of university teaching is to stimulate thinking. Faculty and students seek to acquire the habit of looking at facts critically and objectively, and to pursue the search for truth, and the solution of problems diligently and faithfully, without seeking to distort the facts, or to pervert them in the service of any ideology or doctrine or official dogma. It is in order to help students to be able to consider the facts from various points of view that it has been advocated that courses should be devised to give them the opportunity to become acquainted with the different methods, approaches and values of the humanities, the arts, and the natural and social sciences. The aim is to draw out, and inspire their full intellectual development, and to help them to cultivate the maturity of judgment which they must have for playing their roles in the African scene.

The discussions on manpower needs have shown the part the universities are expected to play in the training of the higher level manpower needed for administration and for social and economic development. It is higher education that will determine the extent to which the potentialities of Africa become actualities, for it controls a nation's development in all fields, economic, political, and military. The engineers, doctors, scientists, administrators and other personnel on whom a nation's economic growth and social progress depend are trained at the institutions of higher education.

It has been apparent, however, that if universities are to attain their ultimate objective, the development of the quality of individual and social life, they must be something more than training centres of the production skills of high level manpower. They must do more than train men and women to be just technicians. They are expected to inculcate in their students a sensitive awareness of the community of which they are members: of its needs, and of the service they can and should render to it. It is the graduates who will give leadership in all walks of life, in the villages and towns and nations of Africa. This requires that they should not only be highly trained men and women, but also educated men and women. They should be good human beings. To this end, a university has the responsibility of inculcating a sense of values. It should be concerned with the development not only of skills and intellect, but also of character. A university must have something to offer to guide men and women how they should live. In the last analysis, its role, as stated above, is to promote a certain quality of individual life, and a certain quality of social life, marked by an intelligent, moral and spiritual appreciation and active pursuit of what is true and beautiful and good. In the conditions of Africa, university education cannot be separated from the fundamental questions: what sort of human being, what sort of society?

VIII. EDUCATION FOR WHAT?

We have noted that all the countries of Africa are making efforts to build a new society, and that they all emphasise the raising of standards of living as an urgent task. This emphasis, however, tends to becloud the ultimate goal. There has been a tendency to see development solely in materialist terms — in roads, harbours, buildings, factories, and the like; and this in turn tends to obscure the fact that the aim for securing these things is to create the environmental conditions which will give every individual the best chance of developing his talents and personality to the fullest extent possible, so that he may be as good a human being and citizen as he can be. The tacit postulate of the argument of this book is that economic policy must be based on respect for human dignity and freedom and on a concept of citizenship in a free society.

Further, economic development should aim not only at raising standards of living, but also at achieving social justice. This implies a narrowing of the gap between those who are very well-off, and those who are very poor. African nationalism is fundamentally a spiritual revolution; it is a striving to achieve human dignity, freedom and social justice, and the acceptance as equals in the family of nations. Its case has a moral justification.

Education is one of the principal media through which

95

these goals can be achieved. What is needed is an educational philosophy with a total view of the individual and a total view of society, in its complex network of relations. What the policies of former Colonial Powers lacked was this comprehensive view of education. Their policies were piecemeal, directed towards short term objectives. They did not assume responsibility for the total evolution of society. They were not nationals fired by visions of the future of their colonial possessions as independent, selfrespecting nations living on terms of equality with their own. Education must be lifted out of the grooves they carved for it. It is apparent that what Africa is seeking is a philosophy of education that has a total view of man and society; one that is rooted in the past, but is also attuned to the revolution of our times, taking account of the transformations now in process, and the new perspectives stretching before us. Education must pass on the heritage of the past, cope with the present, and prepare for the future.

In the first chapter, reference was made to the fact that education in traditional African society prepared the young for the community's way of life. In the modern world, no nation can have the homogeneity or self-sufficiency of a tribal community. National independence must be understood in terms of international interdependence. Training the young for life in a community must now be seen in terms of preparing them for citizenship in a State, in a Continent that is drawing closer together, and in an increasingly inter-dependent world.

The greater awareness of the Continent of Africa is shown in increasing inter-State co-operation. Many examples of this could be given in the field of education. Mauritania's Institute of Islamic Studies founded in 1955 has students from Senegal, Mali, Portuguese Guinea, and Nigeria. The Pedagogic Institute of the University of Dakar serves all French-speaking West Africa. The Universities and University Colleges are admitting more and more students from other African countries besides their own. Fourah Bay College which has for many years taken students from all parts of West Africa had, until recently, more students from other parts of Africa than from Sierra Leone itself. African Governments have been offering scholarships to bring students from other African States to study in the States of the Governments making the awards. In 1958, the Emperor of Ethiopia awarded 200 scholarships tenable in institutions in Ethiopia to African students from other African countries. The first batch included students from Ghana, Liberia, Nigeria, Egypt, Sudan, Tanganyika, Kenya, Uganda and Zanzibar. In an address welcoming them the Emperor said:

"We hope that during your period of study here you will be enabled to observe our people at first hand and to come to know that you are of their same African blood. We shall not fail to send Ethiopian students to schools in other parts of Africa so that the programme of cultural and educational exchanges will extend yet more widely". That extension has been growing. The Liberian Government has offered scholarships to students from other parts of Africa to study in Liberia, and the Ghana Government has offered similar scholarships. The interchange of students is one feature of the growing co-operation among African countries.

Suggestions have been made for the establishment of regional institutions, such as teacher-training colleges and

97

research institutes to serve a number of States jointly, so as to avoid duplications and waste, ensure the best use of the qualified personnel available, and foster understanding and unity. There are Institutes in Europe, such as the International Institute of Social Studies at the Hague, in Holland, which provide a forum specifically for the study of the problems of development in Africa and other developing countries, and attract students from all parts of Africa. There are institutions in America which offer similar facilities. The provision of such institutions in Africa itself would contribute significantly to knowledge of the Continent and to understanding and unity.

Aid from one country in Africa to another is small compared with aid to African countries from outside the Continent. There are numerous examples of international aid to education in Africa from Europe and America and from the United Nations and its agencies, in particular, from UNESCO and the World Health Organisation. To mention a few specific cases: The International Co-operation Administration and American Foundations such as the Carnegie Corporation, the Ford Foundation and the Rockefeller Foundation have made large grants to educational institutions in all parts of Africa for buildings, libraries, equipment, research or the training of teachers. The French Government has provided funds and teachers on a generous scale to her former Colonies and Dependencies. The United States National Council of Churches, the Massachusetts Institute of Technology, the Teachers' College of Columbia University, and smaller Foundations like the Phelpes Stokes Fund and the New World Foundation have taken part in various educational projects, providing grants, fellowships and scholarships, or helped with the establishment or expansion of Colleges, or sponsored new universities. Thousands of students are being trained in educational institutions in countries of both the Western and Eastern blocks. Teachers have voluntarily gone from Britain, France, the United States and Canada, under various schemes and organizations, such as the United States Peace Corps or the International Loans and Educational Aid Programme or Britain's Voluntary Service Organization to help, particularly in secondary schools and colleges. All this international aid in men and money marks a new consciousness of an embryonic international community. It represents the human yearning and striving towards unity and peace. Its progress is barred by prejudices that erect national or racial walls. Education preparing the young for citizenship in Africa must take account of the incipient world community of the twentieth century. It must train for world citizenship and not only for the responsibilities of citizenship in a particular State or nation.

Education is listed among the fundamental rights set out in the Charter of the United Nations. The lack of understanding or appreciation of the difficulties of other nations lies at the root of international tensions. From the very beginning, the framers of the United Nations Charter were aware of this. In the summer of 1945, at the solemn ceremony at which the Charter was adopted by the United States Government, the Chaplain of the Senate gave expression to the desires and hopes of the world in an exalted prayer which ended with the words:

Lord, Our God, in vain we have tried the old way – the way of strife and envy and conflict. Now, with Thy divine help, let us try a new way – with tolerance of diversity – the way of mutual sympathy and fraternal co-operation in the solution of our common problems.

It is the mission of the United Nations and its agencies to inculcate tolerance in diversity, and education is one of its principal instruments, for it lies in the province of education to broaden understanding and teach world citizenship.

The contemporary world has more powerful machines and weapons than any age before it, and there hangs over mankind a pall of fear and anxiety, lest men fail to control the machines and weapons they have made, and start a war which could mean the annihilation of human life. Education cannot neglect the means by which men are taught to control the machines they have made. The means lie in the sphere of morals. World citizenship must have moral and spiritual foundations.

This brings us to consider an aspect of education which cannot be ignored so long as education is accepted as concerned primarily with *being*; with the sort of human beings an educational system helps to mould. Education, formal or informal, as it has come down the ages, through the experience and practice of diverse communities, has always had its roots in religion which provides guidance for moral and spiritual life.

We have noted that the informal education given in traditional African societies instilled reverence, and inculcated a religious attitude to life. It aimed at the development of the young as human beings; it was concerned with standards of conduct and behaviour, whose basis was found in religion. But religious education in Africa today faces the challenge of Christianity and Islam, as well as the challenge of science and technology, and new ideas.

Though the fear of the gods has diminished, and traditional beliefs have been undermined, elements of traditional religions remain, and exercise a tenacious influence in society. Religious education in Africa in the contemporary situation must therefore include the teaching of comparative religions in schools so as to give opportunity for the religious traditions of Africa to be studied and examined, along with Christianity and Islam. The failure to do this has led to much confusion, and to the superficial acceptance as well as rejection of creeds and religions, which have not been adequately studied or understood.

Faced with a similar situation, the Indian University Commission of 1948-9 proposed a comprehensive course in religion. The Commission recommended:

1. That all educational institutions start work with a few minutes of meditation.
2. That in the first year of the Degree Course, the lives of great religious leaders like Gautama the Budha, Confucius, Zoroaster, Socrates, Jesus, Sankar, Ramanuja, Madhava, Mohammad, Kabir, Nanak, Ghandi, be taught.
3. That in the second year some selections of a universal character from the scriptures of the world be taught.
4. That in the third year, the central problems of the philosphy of religion be considered.[1]

The recommendations of the Indian University Commission have two lessons for Africa; first, that the core of studies which should be taken by all students, in school, college, or university, should include religious studies; and second, that for character training, the great religious men of all ages and all countries belong to the common heritage of mankind, for all to draw upon. In Africa special con-

[1] *Indian University Commission, 1948-49*, Vol. 1, p. 303.

sideration should be given to the characters of traditional religions, and Islam and Christianity.

In Islamic communities in Africa, in countries such as North Africa, Egypt, the Republic of Sudan, Gambia, the Somalis, Northern Nigeria, Senegal, Mauritania, and Mali where substantial proportions of the population are Moslems, there is a distinctive Islamic culture. Islam is both a religion and a culture. The rapid changes in political, economic and social life pose new problems for educational systems modelled on the concepts, curricula, and traditional methods of Islamic education. Educating for citizenship in the technological age into which Africa has been ushered calls for special attention to the religious heritage of Islam.

The history of formal education in Africa is tied up with the work of christian missions. In country after country, Liberia, Sierra Leone, Ghana, Nigeria, Uganda, the Rhodesias, Nyasaland, Basutoland, Kenya, the story is the same: christian missionaries pioneered in education, and still play an important role in that field. Missionary education was based on a christian philosophy of education. It was based on the conviction that a pupil would become a better adult and a better citizen if he became a christian. Mission schools therefore propagated the christian religion, and sought to make christians of the people. Since most of the schools in Africa have been run by the christian missions, the majority of the present leaders of Africa, in all walks of life, have been educated in christian schools. They have been nurtured on the teaching that it is from a man's religion that his goodness, both as a man and as a citizen, flows. Those who accept the teaching are furnished with a design for living, provided by the example of Christ.

102

An illustration of this teaching is afforded by the following extract from the Speech Day address given at the Alliance High School, Kikuyu, Kenya, by the headmaster on the 23rd September, 1961:

The school is here to help. It is needed in the new Kenya as well as the old. Its job is to make men, men who will love and serve their God and their country and will have the tools to serve effectively; men who are debtors and not creditors to Kenya, whose eyes are not on what they ought to receive but on what they can contribute, who are glad and grateful givers. The school motto "Strong to Serve" which you will have seen above the entrance to this hall, and on the blazers of the senior boys is new – but it represents an ideal which is old.

We try to hold up a standard, and that standard is christian. I do not say this as a pious appendage to my report or as a gesture of remembrance to the christians who, long ago, founded the school we love. I believe it to be true that today Christ is at the centre of the school. Not all care much about Him; none serve Him as well as he should; yet He is here, seen by all, followed by many. The achievements of which I have spoken, of which I – and, I hope you – are proud, derive from Him.

In considering the ultimate ends of education, Africa cannot ignore the fact that many of its schools have been built on the belief that the full synthesis of all the branches of learning is to be found in religion; the christians would specify that this is to be found in the christian religion; and the Moslems would say in Islam; but they would all agree that education must have a religious basis. The educational heritage of traditional Africa would endorse this, for religion pervaded all aspects of life; in fact, there was no distinction between secular and sacred; all was based on religion. It would thus be ignoring the unanimous testimony of the educational systems which Africa has inherited to push religion to the periphery of education as an optional subject, or one that is a luxurious and not very relevant auxiliary to more urgent demands. There is no rationalist or humanist tradition in Africa, and no one argues that education should be free from religion, for in Africa, ethics has not been divorced from religion, in the tradition which has been handed down; on the contrary, religion provided the sanctions for ethical conduct.

It would be agreed by all, teachers and parents alike, that they want to bring up the young to behave well, to prefer honesty to dishonesty, truth to lies, and to be able to distinguish beauty from ugliness and good from evil, and that this wish would be best fulfilled through a religious education. They would agree that education which has a religious basis helps the development of sound standards of individual conduct and behaviour; and that devotion to some spiritual ideal presented by religion is a source of inspiration in the discharge of public duty. The problem in contemporary Africa is not yet one of an encounter between agnosticism, or humanism or rationalism and religion, but an encounter between different religions: traditional polytheism or animism, and Christianity and Islam.

We have surveyed the role education is expected to play in Africa as she strives for social and economic development, and for entry into the technological age of the twentieth century. Through primary, secondary and vocational schools, technical institutes, colleges, universities and adult education programmes, youth as well as adults must be taught the many trades, occupations, professions and skills necessary for earning a living and for running a modern State. They must be taught to use their hands and their brains to increase national productivity in order that all may enjoy higher standards of living. They must also be made into good human beings and responsible citizens.

Education is, above all, concerned with the development of personality. Decisions on such complex problems of education as whether to have residential colleges or universities, or the structure of degree courses, or the content of curricula, or the ratio of staff to students, and the like, will all depend on the concept of the sort of persons the educational institutions are expected to turn out, and the sort of society that is desired. In the world of the twentieth century, human beings remain as ever the most valuable resource of Africa, and the development of human personality remains the basic task of education.

A philosophy of education must be rooted in the past; and one of the most valuable lessons from Africa's past is that education must be built on spiritual foundations; it must give men and women a religious attitude to life; it must inculcate reverence.

A second lesson is the sensitive awareness of community which was emphasised in the traditional informal methods of education. Besides learning from the past, a philosophy of education must scan the horizons of the future; it must prepare for change. Preparing the young for the future means giving them love and trust in their infancy, so that they may grow loving and trustworthy; cherishing and giving them sympathy within the family and the community so as to strengthen their sense of belonging; preparing them through service and co-operative activity in home and school to accept their social responsibilities in adult life for the wider community of town or nation; inculcating in them the larger sympathy so that they may increasingly become citizens of the world, accepting moral responsibilities for international co-operation; and to this end, providing them with opportunities to fulfil the promise that is in them through the vision and high ideals that religion provides. Youth must be given opportunities to find their own faith in God. The opportunities are given where the older generation faithfully and courageously hand down what they know and believe.

A philosophy of education must also be concerned with the present, with the duties to be done, and the problems that call for immediate solution. This is where training in skills for improving the conditions of life comes in; but since world peace and international co-operation are necessary conditions for economic and social progress, education must also inculcate in men and women a consciousness of the oneness of the human family, so that in mutual respect, free from prejudice and injustice, they may co-operate, in awareness of their common humanity and common destiny, to create a new social order, free from war, and the haunting fear of the annihilation of human life from the surface of the earth.

From whatever angle we approach it, a search for a social philosophy of education must focus attention on the individual human being. He is the hope of the future; the ideals that beckon him will shape the new social order. The ultimate purpose of education is to produce good men and women, and the primary responsibility of the educator and the teacher is to find the best way of doing this. The judgment of many eminent educators, past and present, who have given the matter their attention is that in any branch of knowledge, the way to achieve the best results is to make the pupil or student familiar with the best specimens. A social philosophy of education must hold before men the vision of the best men and the most desirable society, a vision powerful enough to inspire and stir to noble action and conduct.

The grave danger to which we seek to direct serious attention is that in the hectic expansion of educational facilities going on in Africa, attention tends to be limited to meeting immediate needs and solving immediate practical problems, and intermediate objectives are given precedence over the ultimate goals of human dignity and freedom, and social justice and a peaceful world. What is done in education must be seen within the concept of man and society in their totality and inter-relations, and within a vision of the foreseeable future of Africa and the world.

For Product Safety Concerns and Information please contact our EU
representative GPSR@taylorandfrancis.com
Taylor & Francis Verlag GmbH, Kaufingerstraße 24, 80331 München, Germany

* 9 7 8 1 0 3 2 3 5 3 9 1 3 *